Richard St. John Tyrwhitt

Christian Art and Symbolism

with some hints on the study of landscape

Richard St. John Tyrwhitt

Christian Art and Symbolism
with some hints on the study of landscape

ISBN/EAN: 9783337300371

Printed in Europe, USA, Canada, Australia, Japan

Cover: Foto ©Lupo / pixelio.de

More available books at **www.hansebooks.com**

CHRISTIAN ART
AND SYMBOLISM.

CHRISTIAN ART

AND SYMBOLISM,

WITH SOME HINTS ON

THE STUDY OF LANDSCAPE.

BY THE

Rev. R. S^{T.} JOHN TYRWHITT,

FORMERLY STUDENT AND RHETORIC READER OF CHRIST CHURCH, OXFORD.

WITH ILLUSTRATIONS.

LONDON:
SMITH, ELDER & CO., 15, WATERLOO PLACE.
1872.

ADVERTISEMENT.

THESE papers were delivered as Lectures during the Winter and Spring of 1871-2, at Winchester, Bradford, and Halifax. They have been freed, in great measure, from local allusions, and I have reason to hope that they may have enough of general interest to make them acceptable to a tolerably wide circle of readers in their present form.

The autotype of the Delphic Sibyl suffers by reduction, but is sufficient for its purpose. It should be held well off from the eye, like all other small works, till the reader has found his own best focus.

It will be seen that the quotation from Professor Max Müller at p. 204, relating to the spread of the Reformation among the German peasantry and lower clergy, is connected with the beginning, not with the end, of Lecture VI.

R. ST. J. T.

Ketilby, Oxford, 16th April, 1872.

CONTENTS.

Lecture		Page
	Preface, by Professor John Ruskin	ix
I.	Introductory	1
II.	Greek and Christian Art	34
III.	Italian Art-History	70
IV.	Florentine Succession of Painters and History of Symbolism and the Grotesque	106
V.	Rafael and Michael Angelo	139
VI.	Dürer and Holbein	172
VII.	Landscape Sketching	205
VIII.	Poetry of Landscape	237
XI.	Art, Craft, and Schools	262
	Memorial Chart .... *To face page*	292

LIST OF ILLUSTRATIONS.

The Delphic Sybil of Michael Angelo .... *To face Title*

Theseus of Phidias.. *To face page* 41

1. The Vine. Earliest Christian Art 66

2. The Vine. Transitional 67

3. The Vine. Byzantine 67

Byzantine Capital, Ravenna............................ *To face page* 78

Noah—Callixtine Catacomb 128

The Lombard Noah 128

PREFACE.

BY PROFESSOR JOHN RUSKIN.

———◆———

THE writer of this book has long been my friend, and in the early days of friendship was my disciple. But, of late, I have been his; for he has devoted himself earnestly to the study of forms of Christian Art which I have had little opportunity of examining, and has been animated in that study by a brightness of enthusiasm which has been long impossible to me.

Knowing this, and that he was able perfectly to fill what must otherwise have been a rudely bridged chasm in my teaching at Oxford, I begged him to give these lectures; and to arrange them for press. And this he has done to please me; and now that it is done, I am — in one sense — anything but pleased: for I like his writing better than my own, and am more jealous of it than I thought it was in me to be of any good work—how much less of my friend's! I console myself by reflecting, or at least by repeating to myself, and endeavouring to think, that he could not have found all this out if I had not shown him the way. But most deeply and seriously I am thankful for such help, in a work far too great for my present strength;— help all the more precious, because my friend can bring to the investigation of early Christian Art, and its influences, the integrity and calmness of the faith in which it was wrought. Happier than I, in having been a personal comforter and helper of men, fulfilling his life in daily and unquestionable duty; while I have been, perhaps wrongly—always hesitatingly,—persuading myself that it was my duty to do the things that pleased me.

Also, it has been necessary to much of my analytical work that I should regard the Art of every nation as much as possible from their own national point of view; and I have striven so earnestly to realize belief which I supposed to be false, and sentiment which was foreign to my temper, that, at last I scarcely know how far I think with other people's minds, and see with any one's eyes but my own. Even the effort to recover my temporarily waived conviction occasionally fails; and what was once securest to me becomes theoretical, like the rest. But my old scholar has been protected by his definitely directed life, from the temptations of this speculative equity; and I believe his writings to contain the truest expression yet given in England of the feelings with which a Christian gentleman of sense and learning should regard the art produced, in ancient days, by the dawn of the faiths which still guide his conduct, and secure his peace.

On all the general principles of Art, Mr. Tyrwhitt and I are absolutely at one; but he has often the better of me by his acute personal knowledge of men and their ways. When we differ in our thoughts of things, it is because we know them on contrary sides; and often, his side is that most naturally seen, and which it is most desirable to see. There is one important matter, for instance, on which we are thus apparently at issue, and yet are not so in reality. These lectures show, throughout, the most beautiful and just reverence for Michael Angelo, and are of especial value in their account of him: while the last lecture on Sculpture, which I gave at Oxford, is entirely devoted to examining the modes in which his genius itself failed, and perverted that of other men. But Michael Angelo is great enough to make praise and blame alike necessary, and alike inadequate, in any true record of him. My friend sees him as a traveller sees from a distance some noble mountain range, obscure in golden clouds and purple shade; and I see him as a sullen miner would the same mountains, wandering among their precipices through chill of storm and snow, and discerning that their strength was perilous, and their substance sterile. Both of us see truly—both partially; the complete truth is in the witness of both.

The notices of Holbein, and of the English whom he painted, (see especially the sketch of Sir Thomas Wyatt in the sixth lecture), are to my mind of singular value; and the tenor of the book throughout, as far as I can judge, for, as I said, much of it treats of subjects with which I am unfamiliar, so sound, and the feeling in it so warm and true, and true in the warmth of it, that it refreshes me like sight of the things themselves it speaks of. New and vivid sight of them it will give to many readers; and to all who will regard my commendation I commend it; asking those who have hitherto credited my teaching to read these lectures as they would my own; and trusting that others, who have doubted me, will see reason to put faith in my friend.

Pisa, 30th April, 1872.

CHRISTIAN ART

AND

SYMBOLISM.

LECTURE I.

INTRODUCTORY.

THOUGH doing is preferable to talking in all practical sciences, and though more knowledge of art would, probably, be gained by copying an oak branch, or a mossy stone, or a cast of the Torso, under proper inspection, than by reading these papers—still a certain amount of speech is necessary to art now and then; because people require to have their attention faithfully drawn to it. No doubt reading will not make even a competent critic without careful observation of nature, at the least; and some manual skill is felt to be necessary to him, by all the painters on whom he is to express an opinion; partly because it enables him to understand the difficulties they contend with; and partly because it sharpens his powers of observation, and teaches him to appreciate their execution. And appearing here in the character of critic, I should like to introduce what the French call a *pièce justificative*, about that generally-objectionable race of men. Mr. Phœbus says that critics are the men who have failed in art or literature. Balzac said it at first of St. Beuve—and, of course, it annoyed St. Beuve very much, which was all it was intended to do. But none of all the epigrams in Lothair was more delightfully pungent than this saying or quotation, which annoyed a class of men whom all the world is glad to see annoyed, and produced an effect, in the daily and weekly press, like that of firing a blunderbuss into a rookery. But it is quite true. Nobody can be either poet, painter, or critic, till he has made a great many failures, in the first place. Then in art a good second-rate man, well skilled in technicalities, and generally well educated, will be a better critic, on the whole, than a great genius who has enough to do to think his own thoughts without minding his contemporaries, and who frequently refuses to talk about his work at all. But what is failure? Does any man ever succeed in doing all he wants to do as well as it can be done? and does he also succeed in getting all the world to acknowledge his success? Because anything short of that is failure; and in intellectual works of high aim, you never can tell how long a time may be required for success. Then if intellectual success means what I think it does mean, namely, communicating your ideas to other men so as to make them understand you, and think with you; then many men have a great deal of real success, who are failures in point of *éclat* or profit. The fact is, want of success is a varying, uncertain matter, and may be usefully divided into failures to do anything good, and failures to get anything good. Let us be thankful, at all events, that the many of us who fail in the latter way are not necessarily of those who fail in the former. But in both poetry and painting, almost every man may be said to reach his point of failure. He may use his capacity to the utmost, but at last he can do no more, he finds something absolutely beyond him. A man may write a small volume of good verse with some passion, some new thought and scholarly English in it; but such a person fails as a poet if he can't go on with it, and keep it up, and express the thoughts of his life in rhythmic and musical form,

I daresay many well-taught ladies are capable, like the mighty men of old in the Apocrypha, of inventing musical tunes, or composing a pretty air now and then. But that is very different from the sustained production of Schumann, whose suffering life was endurable only because it expressed its whole sad course in harmonies. Quantity must tell: there are hogsheads of claret, and there are sample bottles. Consider the amount of writing which Carlyle and Browning went through—both of them being men who put their hearts into everything, never spared labour, never gave except of their best —consider the vast productions of those two minds, before either obtained what is called success. Why they are not successful men now in one sense; for neither of them has got or been made anything, except in university distinctions, and such like barren honour; but I do not suppose their admirers will think they need much more.

Again, it is of the nature of failure not to improve as one goes on, not to gather strength with years and labour. I suppose, in fact, every man who combines common sense with high aspiration, must have the full sensation of failure when he looks at his own deeds, and the sum of his ways, and compares them with his ideal; or even with what they might actually have been. I am sure every good Christian must feel thus: assuredly, it is better in the end for a man to own himself an unprofitable servant. But, in painting, I should be inclined to say a man has failed, and died away in the race, when he begins to repeat himself, and multiply his works for money; not pressing on to do better things, or even to do things better. Many men, highly successful as far as money goes, I should call failures, because they are untrue to their genius. Life is a long race, and the stayers have the best of it after all: those who run the longest, who continue to have and to follow fresh inspirations, doing their best for the best's sake. It is this pressing on to the prize unseen: it is this steady pursuit of the ideal: it is this sense of the craftsman's honour: it is this desire to do work, if possible, better than ever it was done before, or if not, better than one ever yet did it oneself, which brings the pursuit of Art into such close relation with the Spiritual or Religious life. No doubt that Art is the working of an excellent spirit in man: it needs faith in that which is unseen: it is the pursuit of a good which never will be reached in this world; and so far it is a phase of spiritual life. I cannot avoid noticing its close analogy with that universal, spiritual race or progress which is open to the weak, as well as the mighty, and which bids all alike, so run that they may obtain.

In a few words, it is quite true that it is easier to talk than to do, and that many people talk and criticise who cannot draw, or who have tried and failed; or who have not made progress enough to give them proper judgment or authority. You cannot stop them in a free country; and the real cure for bad criticism is to encourage competent and honest criticism. I never had the honour of being connected with any newspaper; but I presume that if the public did not demand sharp spiteful articles, journalists would not write them; and that the best way of discouraging facetious ignorance, is not to read it. But a poet may view a painter as a brother poet or creator, and analyse or criticise the thoughts he expresses, to excellent purpose. Rogers's tribute to Michael Angelo, and Browning's analysis of Fillippo Lippi are of the highest artistic value, though neither of them can be called practical painters. Their criticisms express intelligent sympathy with another's thoughts, and they make no comment on his technical methods.

The fact is, all criticism is a free fight; but when it gets serious, and "the bills step forth, and the bows go back," the Anonymi and Pseudonymi disperse. When men who are not ashamed of their names meet in earnest, right is generally done, after some smiting. But there is no doubt that if you are to criticise the technique of pictures, you ought, at least, to have tried to draw : because nothing else can give you an idea, either of the difficulty of the subject, or of its interest, or of the immense difference between works of fine hand, perception, and purpose, and slovenly, coarse, or false work. For quick work is often most delicate; and one of the most laborious and consummate workmen who ever lived, Holman Hunt, is also most rapid in his execution.

And, indeed, you cannot really observe, without drawing—I mean that an ordinary person commonly occupied cannot. Wordsworth did so, with pre-Rafaelite accuracy, when he wrote of the beauty of the daisy's star-shaped shadow "thrown on the rude surface of the naked stone." Scott was a noble colourist; and in the humbler walks of life I know farm-servants, keepers, and gillies who make excellent use of those habits of watching the outer face of nature, which their life enforces on them; they are naturalists, if not artists, in feeling. But no one can for a moment doubt the use of drawing to a naturalist, because it not only enables him to record his observations, but helps him to observe minutely and correctly. All the Arts and Sciences depend more from year to year on illustration. When you have seen a picture of a thing, your idea about it is better than it would have been from mere description—that is truism. All who are used to drawing will agree that you see very much more in a thing when you begin to draw it, than you saw before you began. And anybody who has never attempted to draw a natural object will find, whenever he does so, that the humblest bit of nature has more in it than he thought. I suppose that a hen's egg is a very simple and humble natural object: it is one of the first things generally given pupils to copy in light and shade. Before you begin to draw it you just see it is an egg, and hope it is a fresh one. When you begin, you notice first its whiteness, the oval line which limits that whiteness, and beauty in that oval; then the rounding or structural shade of that oval whiteness; then the cast shadow, and darker objects behind, which produce the effect of whiteness, and the gradations which produce the effect of rounding on your eye. The attempt at imitating all these qualities makes you see them more and more clearly. That is a lesson of observation by means of drawing, and it cannot be had without drawing. A great deal is said about the hand obeying the eye ; but the fact is, that a good hand is like a good servant, and educates the eye in its post of command. There is nothing like touch; all skilled work depends upon it ; it is the result of harmonious action between the hand, which feels and presses, and the eye which watches and reports simultaneously to the spirit. That is why copies are inferior to originals ; because in the latter you have the master's hand and eye working together in the action of self-expression. "In Italy," says Nathaniel Hawthorne (*Transformation*, p. 95), "it is not quite satisfactory to think that a sculptor has very little to do with the power of actually chiselling the marble. There is a class of men who do it for him with exquisite mechanical skill. In no other art, surely, does genius find such effective instruments, and so happily relieve itself of the drudgery of actual performance. The admiration which our artists get for buttons, button-holes, shoe-ties, and neckcloths, at our present epoch of taste, makes a large share of their renown. It would be abated if we were generally aware that the sculptor can claim no credit for these pretty things. They are not his work, but that of some nameless machine in human shape." This passage is, I believe, literally true, and its quiet irony shows what a good art-critic the author would have made—and indeed actually was—without technical knowledge. Of course, the hand of the master is everything. Who would ever think of polishing the rough chiselling from the face of Michael Angelo's Day or Twilight?

Artistic touch is really the expression of one of the most wonderful works of God; of the union, or united action, of thought and living matter on other matter. That great statue called the Thought of Michael Angelo — the misnamed Duke Lorenzo — that thought streamed through his fingers wonderfully, and ate away the marble till the block became a spiritual thing to all intents and purposes. I could not fancy its being done through another man's fingers, nor could it be.

But now I think it is time to give some reason for the hope that is in us, that Art is a really and practically good thing for us. I say in, and for us, for I think, as lawyers say, that the court is with me. So it is in a sermon; and yet how difficult it is, how truly a gift given one, hardly to be commanded of one's own will, to say any good thing which one's neighbour will render into deed? And how impossible it is to put subtlety into anybody's eye, or to give the craftsman's touch to the nerves of the hand, by merely talking or writing! But as to the good of Art—as to the reason why many of us should take to drawing, and all of us encourage all men to do so. Our reasons for it are our hopes from it, or, which is the same thing, the wants which press us to it. And, in the first place, we want, and through art we hope for, more knowledge for our selves, keener perception, more invention, more freshness, more geist, as philosophers say, a higher and better spirit, as Christians say; greater vigour of existence — we want that got into our measure of days here—

> 'Tis life whereof our nerves are scant;
> More life, and fuller—that we want.

By we, I mean every one of us. Some of us are weary of work; some of us are bored with want of work. I do not want to exalt one class at the expense of the other—working too hard is sometimes a fault, and at best it is a misfortune. But being bored really consists in wanting suitable employment for one's energies—sometimes in having deprived oneself of it, or got on wrong employment. Art is a practical subject of thought for all of us who have leisure for culture, or who are engaged in the culture of others' minds or their own employment. And I want all, or a good many here, to reflect how Art in its various branches may be a right employment for them, and for those whom they guide or influence. To which end let us have a few divisions and distinctions for clearness' sake. I do not know that they are good, but they help to express my meaning.

What I understand by Art, after twenty or thirty years at it, is that it *originates* as an energy or activity of the spirit of man, set in him by the Father of all spirits as a means of delight in the days of his vanity; and that it *consists in* search for and production of beauty. Then, as perfect beauty, or the idea of beauty, is here unattainable, the pursuit of it is of the nature of aspiration; incessant, delightful, insatiable, unresting. The work of a perfect artist would be "like a perpetual fountain to a perpetual thirst."* I shall give cautions enough against overwork and want of method, I hope, when we come to practical remarks. In art as in other things, *surtout, point de zèle*. What I mean here is that what we call Fine Art never ceases to aspire. Poets, painters, musicians, and good

* *Romola.*

craftsmen will follow their craft, like Tennyson's crew, for ever:—

> They know the merry world is round,
> And they may sail for evermore.

Then I should say, that Art divides itself into Ideal Art, pursuit of pure beauty, and applied Art, which uses beauty for educational or even commercial purposes. The word ideal is generally objected to. I have not refreshed my memory about all the metaphysics I once swallowed in connection with that word. Let this suffice for us now. Ideal Art is the pursuit of your idea, by your will and intellect, or spirit; therefore it is a spiritual pursuit, in the wider sense. It is spiritual or religious, in the more limited sense, when you are pursuing an idea of the highest class; that is to say, one which refers to Divine or spiritual natures above your own. In such thought and the works which result from it, the spiritual and the ideal are the same thing. But the pursuit of such an ideal must be made with absolute sincerity and singleness of purpose. It may be said that sacred Art is applied Art; because it is applied to teaching, though of the highest subject. In that case let us say that applied Art may be also spiritual. You may say that Angelico's skill is *applied* to sacred work; but he applies it with absolute sincerity, to set forth that which he believed. His art is a pursuit of the ideal, in that he pursued the chief good, the source of all ideas or forms of beauty and of truth. All sacred Art, insofar as it is truly sacred, is the expression of this, that a man has an idea of seeing and a desire to see the face of God, whatever those words mean; that he longs for the Beatific Vision, and expresses his longing. In so doing he is taught to gather from the visions or sights of this earth, and to project again from himself, images of spiritual beauty, which he thinks may be symbolic of the object of his longing. That kind of work is not for many, and those who are marked for it will be led to it. I say nothing of it here except that it is wholly ideal because it is spiritual, seeking the greatest idea, or spiritual fact, which can exist. The ideal and the spiritual, or the beautiful and the spiritual, meet at last, as two parallel lines of railroad seem to meet; below the horizon, and in perspective very far away.

But Art may be applied to education and right spiritual development, and that is the application we have to do with here. So used, it becomes ideal according as a man is enabled to throw his own spirit or personality into it according to his powers and perceptions; according to the excellence of the spirit that is given him. Ideal means spiritual, if it means anything. We have had it explained to us, quite truly, that Art is not essentially moral or didactic — the rules, the study, and the practice of Art are not. A very good man may be a very bad painter, and blue and yellow still make green in the most profoundly immoral hands; nor can the rules of perspective, or the nature of truths or colours be modified, by the character of those who use them. But the men who obey the rules and pursue the study are moral agents, and the work they produce is moral or immoral accordingly. For all honest work is morally good, and you may take the word of Hooker and Butler for it: —"The ways of well-doing are in number as many as the paths of human action." Shakspeare, we are told, is not didactic. He did not think of making somebody in *Othello* observe like a chorus, throughout, or at the end of the play, that it is wrong to tell lies about a lady, or to smother her with a pillow. Scott is not didactic; he did not improve Torquil of the Oak into a homily, or conclude the *Heart of Mid Lothian* with any earnest exhortations about filial or sisterly affection. But in this Scott and Shakspeare-bepraising age let some of us do more than praise; let us read *Othello* again, or go into the character of Jeanie Deans. Art, we said, was the expression of man's delight, or wondering comprehension of God's work. Let the tenderness and truth which delighted the soul of the Edinburgh lawyer have their result on your spirit. Is the effect of Jeanie Deans moral or immoral, or neither? It was written that Shakspaere should delight in the wonders of the heart of man. Read *Othello;* let some of that tempest of passion blow loud through the chambers of your brain; the love that is as strong as death; the jealousy cruel as the grave—will that degrade your soul, or purify it, or neither? You may feel with Desdemona if you like, or with Iago if you like; but not being an idiot you cannot help doing one or the other; and if you do one, Shakspeare is morally good for you, and if you do the other, it is the contrary. Call his work undidactic if you will; but never say it does not deal with spirit. We won't have any more about Art moral or Art immoral. The sun is not strictly moral, for he is made to shine on the just and unjust alike; the world is far from moral; but we hope that it may be the way to heaven.

But, after all, our subject is *applied* Art. We have to consider that it may be applied to common people, things, and uses, and may be made to pay commercially. There is no doubt it is made to pay.

How, in this practical England, plain men go straight to their work of money-getting, and pictorially advertise hotels, and cattle food, and patent safes, and grand pianos; and how Art is employed in clothing our railway stations with cheerful and practical hideousness—while we, who want more culture and spiritual life, are puzzled and dubious about using Art for spiritual or intellectual purposes. There is not a primary school in England which is painted with the history of England; there is no public school ornamented with anything more instructive than carvings of their own names by the youthful pocket-knives of British worthies. It used to be so at Westminster, and I daresay it is so still, and elsewhere also. And then you are told how interesting it is to have these Graffite of men afterwards renowned; like Sinaitic inscriptions of wanderers through the howling wilderness of school. How useful it must be for idle little boys to know that their great ancestors were as idle as they were. How absurd, how profane, how heterodox, how very slow, how generally improper, would it be to have a fresco of Marathon, or Hastings, or Cressy, or Trafalgar, instead of the incised autograph of the distinguished little Jawkins, who afterwards became a cabinet minister. And all the while we are illustrating all our books of history and antiquities, not very well, it is true, but usefully. I say not well in general, because, if you take up good educational books, like Smith's Dictionaries, you will find the illustrations, on the whole, inferior to the letter-press, on which highly competent men have been employed. Whereas if you take up, for instance, Dr. Rolleston's last work, you will see that the illustrations are of first-rate accuracy; which is all that he requires of them. But, in fact, all phrontisteria, or places where thought or meditation is done, should be illustrated to assist thought. Decoration with ideas is as cheap as decoration without, and the painted symbol often conveys ideas with greater power and vividness than the printed symbol. Letters can tell you that sunsets are pensive and battles tumultuous; but the painter can give you a vision of your own, a share in the press of combat or the calm of evening; letters describe an event, a picture makes you remember it.

Now, there is a "sourd" objection to the use of Art in the English mind, and it is based on its misuse. We have all heard of and seen demoralizing Art, and high technical skill and sense of beauty are often alike abused by it, as in Correggio's Antiope, which may be taken as the type of the great sin of a great painter. But it is not, after all, necessary now to inquire about whether Art be a good thing or not, or to show that the abuse of a good thing does not necessarily make it a bad thing. I have no gift for denunciation, and am quite unequal to expressing my opinion about sensual abuse of pictorial power. Let us extend Dante's advice about such things. He said, "Look, and pass on." I say pass on, and don't look. Ignore Sir Pandarus and all his works. Our question is not of the abuses, but of the humbler uses, of Art; and I cannot help feeling that these are, for the time, its chief uses. What will it do—not so much for those who have every other means of education, as for those who have no other? Is there any good in it for those many who say—who will show us any good? Most of us are aware of a certain monotony, plainness, dulness, ugliness, in our middle-class life. What is to be said of the poor and struggling life of England? A great deal is always being said of it; and much of that is so utterly painful, so distressing and overwhelming, that many able persons seem to despond altogether about the usefulness, or rather the possibility, of artistic pleasure and enjoyment of beauty for the majority of our population. Yet I hold that the true patron of Art, and the true source of Art, is an educated people; it is not a well-principled despot here, or a kind rich man of culture there, who can promote Art, as it is called, in a national way. It can only be done by the gradual education of numbers into appreciation and desire of beauty as a comfort to their weary lives. It may be in vain, but personally I hope to work for this.

This is what Lord Derby says, following the line of thought opened twenty years ago by the present Slade Professor at Oxford. What was visionary then is statesmanlike now, but it was as true then as it is now. Hear Lord Derby—he begins with the usual facts and calculations about the superiority of French Art instruction and manufactories, based on the Exhibition of 1867. He says that our neglect of Art in every department of industry makes us mere hewers of wood and drawers of water for other nations; and he shows that local exertion in this matter is better than State aid, in which I quite agree. State aid is really held out to us through the Science and Art Department. Then he goes on—"We live in a very busy, not in a very beautiful part of England.* If the country continues to prosper, these districts will be still busier and still less pleasant to see. More than half our population now live in great towns, and they are the ugliest, as well as the biggest, in Europe.

* Spoken at Liverpool.

Can it be a good thing for generations to grow up, one after another, seeing nothing, except on some rare holiday, but what is squalid, dirty, and mean ? It seems to me a cruelty to give a man, by artistic training, a keen sense and appreciation of natural beauty, and then to set him down to live in the centre of Liverpool ; and still more of such places as the great towns on the coalfield. Is it a law of nature that things must always continue so ? I do not see it. The smoke which shuts out the sky, the chemicals which destroy vegetation, the unlovely sights which in any one of these towns meet you at every turn, are all preventible evils, and at no great cost. If I were to look at it in an artistic point of view only, I should not be very sanguine of your being able to develop a real and popular love for Art in places where all natural beauty is driven away and destroyed."

There is a tone of despair in this : and I do not suppose that we, who wish to possess and impart to others below us, that delight in God's works which is the essence of Art, shall live to see it very widely extended. But the feeling and care for Art, which induces people to read essays of this unpromising title, is really a call to Art as well as to read ; to help the instruction of others, as well as learn oneself ; to use and press on every means and every measure by which instruction may be more widely spread. I have never had clerical duty in a great manufacturing town; perhaps, I could not have done it. I have often thought so, in passing northward by rail to Highland or Yorkshire moors, rejoicing in prospects of an autumn holiday and the "glory of shooting-jackets." And, to do myself justice, it spoils many days of my holiday to see the smoke of the torment of cotton and iron, hanging over league after league, and county after county; going up always like incense to the god of false political economy, over-production and haste to be rich. But I have fourteen years' close experience of the habits of English people, small tradesmen, workmen, their wives and children —in a large parish in Oxford. And I should say, considering the hard realities of their life, you need never be the least afraid of giving them too keen appreciation of natural beauty. Teach them first that it really exists for them. First catch your pupils, by using pictures in your primary schools, and making the rudiments of drawing a part of your primary education, accessible if not compulsory. When you have trained a few good lads, you will have taught them to look for beauty—you will have taught the cats the way to the cream. If you took a man out of Sheffield, and educated him for years as an artist at Florence, he probably wouldn't like Sheffield when he had to go back. But we want to teach some rudiments at home in Sheffield. What we are desirous of, I hope, is that there should be good schools of design, and models of beautiful work, and flowers and still life, even means of study from nature, in all the great grim towns on the coal-field. Mechanical drawing and conventional design can be taught to any mechanic's son who is a good steady lad; and they are a means of advancement. They are not Art, but they bring him within range of Art; he begins to see form and colour; if he has feeling and spirit he will want to make experiments in them; he will begin to compare his Art-school work with nature. And when you have done that for any, you have given him the key of a new world of his own; an open door is before him and none can shut it. Drawing is like sport, the pursuit is the object; the change, exercise, interest, does the good. I speak here as a parson, as a practical psychologist and dealer in culture. You cannot have a city of draughtsmen; you cannot have a population of æsthetic tinkers, as I was once reminded, I remember. But a man who can mend a kettle properly, or take off a shaving in good form, is probably capable of drawing if he is capable of admiring; and you must begin to teach him and his by giving him something to admire. Open galleries and collections; public gardens and window gardens; parks, playgrounds, excursion trains—all these things help the pupils of your Art-school, and bring you in more of them.

No doubt there is a drawing instinct, and some have more of it, others less. Those who have not got it are open to other means of culture besides Art; and we must accept the means that are given us. Here we have a national system of examination in Science and Art, stimulating instruction; do let us work it as well as we can. The Science Department, as a means of culture, will attract the majority; yet drawing is a part of Science. Practically, a certain number of pupils in our schools will tell themselves off to the more artistic pursuit of drawing, and make it an amusement or even a profession. Let all the pupil-teachers, and best pupils of our primary schools, be rewarded with free tickets for Science or Art school-teaching. I have a large parish primary school; not a bad one, thanks to a good school-master. And I have a pretty large draft of good boys in the Oxford Art School: some of them do pretty well, and that is, and always must be, encouragement enough to continue the system. For parents and friends take interest in their children's drawings, to an extent you cannot over-estimate. In short the Art-school is a means of culture; and I will believe in a mechanic's being over-cultivated, and distressed by being taught to draw—when I see such a man, and not before. I *have* known a workman of great artistic power take to drinking; but I know several others who do nothing of the kind, and he would have done so all the same if he had continued a plain bricklayer, without learning to carve!

Now, to have Art popularized, and made a means of culture for the people, it is practically necessary that it should be made to pay; and that too by the patronage of the people. That is to say, Art wants a patron always; and popular Art wants the patronage of the more numerous classes. This is why we ought to respect commercial or paying Art; because it is popular Art, because it brings uncultivated people within Art-range. If you get beautiful things into the common market, you get them into common life, and then people begin to make progress from them. You want to get men into the Art-world, because they will find comfort and culture there; and you must have accessible means for them. Their life is ugly and you want it to be not so ugly. This is what our many Art-schools and kindred societies wish to do—to get cheaply at the right sort of cup and platter, and the right sort of wall-paper and window-curtain; and the right coloured carpet, and the truest woodcuts, and lithographs, and photographs of the worthiest subject; finally, the picture, mosaic and statue of the highest aim. We want to get the best work into the best place, or fullest circulation. Right patronage blesses him that gives as well as him who receives. I think, if I could get up a popular feeling for simple landscape, or still life, or well-shaped crockery, all down a back street, so that workmen and costermongers should spend pence on small things really fit to be seen: that would be the patronage of Art that I desire to see. I want buyers from back slums; and next after that, I should like to see an intelligent search for originality and sincerity in work, on the part of richer people, who can buy pictures. Of this, perhaps, hereafter; but it may encourage us all to consider (in spite of the feeling, and the misgivings, which do Lord Derby so great honour), how vigorous patronage is given to Art in the great manufacturing cities. They often buy the wrong picture; the practice of their Art-schools is capable of improvement. I know the evils of our Art-school system of competition; they have been lately pointed out in *Fors*

Clavigera: our Science and Art teaching may not be the best conceivable; but anyhow it is there. It is accessible, it gives England a means of culture sorely needed, and may extend a happy influence into a low stratum. Do not let us be afraid of æsthetic tinkers, if only we can get them. I fear some minds may have a lurking objection to æsthetic clergy: and I may just say for myself that I consider my own pursuit of Art is justifiable, since it is not inconsistent with much work as priest, preacher, almoner and visitor; and I do sincerely look on it as a means of popular culture and education. The differences of social life, I well hope, are felt very keenly at the higher end of it, by those who have all the advantages. Can it be that there is a means of imparting some of our best and highest enjoyment to people below us, who are, after all, people exceedingly like ourselves? Have we a chance of doing any spiritual good to our own people? of opening the eyes of the unseeing to delights which God meant for them? If we can help to do this, our life will not have been in vain.

Let me recapitulate a little here. It is satisfactory to persuade oneself that a connection exists between Art and English life, and if I can make others think so too, I shall be infinitely delighted. This paper began by depreciating mere talk about Art, in favour of practice. Nevertheless it was said, in effect, that criticism, or talk about Art, must go on; we can't be all silent painters, and the greatest painters require intelligent criticism to interpret them and explain the value of their work; and criticism may be highly intelligent without technical knowledge. However, on the other hand, it seemed your criticism or enjoyment of all Art work will be so infinitely improved by your learning to draw that you had much better do so. Then, I went on to say, Art is a spiritual thing; man's use of the gift of the Spirit of God, in order to express his delight in God's work, is Art. The mere copy or imitation of nature is not enough, it must have the stamp of the human mind which produced it, and it must bear the trace of intelligence or of delight. Some seeds are sown by traversing the bodies of birds, and so Fine Art cannot grow, unless its germs, the forms of natural beauty, pass through the mind or invention of a man. Fine Art is not imitation, but intelligent, imaginative or delighted record.

Then Art was considered as an energy or pursuit, and first, Ideal: the pursuit of absolute beauty. Of this spiritual beauty is the highest form; so that the Ideal and the Spiritual coincide at last in regions which man may seek but not reach in this world. Secondly, we said Art might be applied to uses, especially to those of instruction and education. This opened the question, whether it might not be our duty to encourage the learning and the practice of Art by all means in our power. We saw that a national system of education is in use among us; it seemed that though it be imperfect, it will in all probability amend itself; and above all it is *there*. Further, Art is really at last represented at our Universities. I cannot see why it should not be encouraged also by University prizes, and that may come later. Then we glanced at the need of national education; of teaching men, first, that they are not beasts (which necessarily involves religious or spiritual information about themselves); secondly, of supplying them with such fact-knowledge, manual dexterity, capacity of sound thought, right emotion, and mental culture in general, as Christian men ought to have. It was said Art is a means to this end; that its pursuit gives peace, independence, the power of contemplation and observation, and delight therein; in fact it makes a man free of a world of his own. We saw the blessing this might be to so many of our race; and asserted the possibility of their possessing or enjoying some forms of beauty, even in their ugliest dwellings. It was acknowledged that great efforts are making to that end, and something was said of public collections and various means of bringing the sight of beauty within the reach of all people. And I meant to convey my impression that the present work of the Department of Science and Art is and will be of great value to us; as it will open a kind of career for energetic lads, workmen's sons who live within poverty mark. I said that boys of capacity in primary schools ought to have gratuitous teaching in the Science and Art schools, and said that we manage it in Oxford. It is of great consequence to unite denominational primary education with the State system as closely as possible; and that is done by giving the best boys and pupil-teachers in primary schools a chance in these State examinations. And we need not and must not be afraid of over-educating or developing too much artistic power and tenderness in our great manufacturing towns. A mechanic of genius is like a prince who has a genius; his skin is thinner than other men's in his position; he must have the advantages of refinement and pay their price. But if you can make a mechanic something of an artist in a hideous town, he will be the better for it: and see if he does not make the town less hideous. Great efforts are made in Manchester and elsewhere; and therefore, from time to time, great mistakes. But the great merchants do buy pictures of their own choice, and the clerks and workmen do work at the schools with their own hands. They are producing quantities of minor works of conventional or applied art—copies, patterns, and designs. In so doing they are well and happily employed, they are learning to feel the want of natural beauty in Manchester, no doubt; but they are also learning to rejoice in it whenever they get out of Manchester, and to record their delight in it, and bring it home. And then, in multiplying good designs, with which the schools supply them, they are bringing beauty within the reach of the people who want it most. Of course minor and auxiliary arts advance with drawing and painting. Etching, engraving, architectural carving, photography; these are all branches of the same thing. But there should be always open access to works of higher aim; or at least there is a higher class of popular art which should always be within everybody's reach in large towns. Small public galleries or collections should be formed, attached perhaps to the art-schools, but open to the public—to the ragged public—boys and girls and all. They should consist mainly of landscapes, perhaps by Stanfield, Harding, by Brett, Inchbold, or

Richardson and Birkett Foster, Alfred Hunt or Powell, Jackson or Duncan,—one specimen of each of these masters might be bought and kept in permanent exhibition in all the big towns in England, and if that were done it would be a blessing to many a carpenter, and tailor, and navigator. Don't think these fellows cannot admire because you won't let them see anything but what is ugly. A great northern city is sure to be crowded often with people who have seen better days and green fields—you are not likely to go wrong in setting any kind of landscape within their reach. Blake lived his life without any sight of the higher beauties of nature; and Turner spent a fourth of his in searching for landscape subjects within reach of Old Maiden Lane. Wordsworth created the taste by which his work could be enjoyed. Surely it is a high enough occupation for any of us to create or aid the faculties by which the works of God can be enjoyed.

There are a few lines of verse I have written down here, to the purpose that we ought to do something for posterity, in a country where our forefathers have done so much for us. Mr. Browning has been looking on Nature in glory. He, by his Art, expresses his delight in God's work, and so he thinks of England and history, and the making of her history. He is off the coast of Spain at evening, and thus he says:—

Nobly, nobly, Cape St. Vincent to the Eastward died away;
Sunset ran, one glorious blood-red, reeking into Cadiz Bay;
Bluish 'mid the burning water, full in face Trafalgar lay;
In the dimmest North-East distance dawned Gibraltar, grand and grey:
"Here and here did England help me—how can I help England?" Say
Whoso turns, as I at evening turn to God, to praise and pray,
While Jove's planet rises yonder, silent over Africa.

LECTURE II.

GREEK AND CHRISTIAN ART.

I AM only going to refer to a short period of Greek history to-day—from Marathon in 490 to the beginning of the Peloponnesian War in 432-1, or its end in 405. I hope it is not too much if I ask you to remember that that is the period of the great glory of Athens and the life of Phidias, in whom Greek sculpture centres. I have constructed a scheme or chart to assist your memory of these lectures; and we shall get through its first part to-day. Ageladas, Phidias, Myron—these men were handsome flesh-and-blood fellows in white or yellowish tunics, with white or purple-striped cloaks like plaids; and so were all their friends. Some of them wore golden grasshoppers in their hair. They were men, and not names only: and once upon a time they might all have been seen chipping away in a moderately-sized, oblong-square, bright, lowish building on the top of a hill. Call that hill the

Acropolis, the fortress or high place of Athens; call the building the Parthenon—it is the dwelling of a certain Maiden Wisdom, named of men Athene. It has a pediment, a low gable in front supported on columns; in that pediment, with others, were the statues now in the Elgin room at the British Museum, which those photographs reproduce in part. Within is the dread Wisdom in ivory and gold, golden ægis and Gorgon over her dark thundery purple robes: "nor wants there in her hand what seems both spear and shield." Round the friezes are the combats of Amazons and heroes, and the triumph of olive-crowned knights of Athens, and their horses would delight Yorkshire as well as they did Attica. All is white and gold and faint tinting, perhaps, on the marble, and clear warm shadow over white and gold. The sky is deep azure to-day, as it was yesterday, as it will be to-morrow, except in the rose of dawn and the flames of sunset. You look over a glittering town, and a plain of grey olive, and corn, and cypress, and ivy, and poplar, and willow, and reed, the delight of Greeks, in the line of the fast-rising long walls, down to the busy port and the triremes, and the blue profound sea and its islands. Think now that Pericles and Aspasia were in the many-coloured crowd which filled the Parthenon this morning; that Æschylus came up with his brother Ameinias, the maimed captain of Salamis; that Sophocles was there, and Anaxagoras, perhaps, conspicuous for his absence; and that a sad young man named Aristophanes was to be seen, and, perhaps, a beautiful youth called Alcibiades, and a very ugly friend of his by the name of Socrates—all these and their race have one thought—to clothe the city of their delight with her garment of victory. For they are the men of Marathon, and the hard sea-fights of the Artemisium and Salamis; and of Platæa and Mycale, and last, of the Eurymedon. They have saved Greece again and again, in spite of herself: they have won such fame as never yet was won, since the Golden Fleece was brought home from Colchis. They are a free state governed by its best man, Pericles, son of Xanthippus; they have got the right man in the right place, and till he dies he will rule them rightly. But they do not love him, or any master; anarchy is coming on them; they show their teeth at him as they dare, and tear his friends away from him one by one; and Phidias will die in prison for his reward, the year before the ruinous war begins. Jerusalem was not the only city that slew her prophets—or Hebrews then, or Puritans afterwards, the only murderers of poet sages.

In any retrospect of Art, however sketchy, it is necessary to go back to its earlier and greatest documents—that is to say, to the earlier Greek models, with Phidias as their leading representative. And the subject of the relations of Greek and Christian Art involves some discussion of the relations of Greek and Christian life. It must do so if Art has anything to do with the spirit or life of man. And as there is no compressing a matter of this kind within the limits of one brief lecture, this paper will be only a sort of dash or raid into the subject, bringing a little knowledge out of it, with rapid retreat from the overpowering forces of what I do not know.

Now, to an artist, merely as a man who delights in seeing and recording natural beauty, the great difference between Greek and modern Anglo-Christian life would be that Art and Nature met in Greek life, and do not meet in ours. The Greek saw enough of beauty to know how much it is worth. Our life, artistically speaking, is a continual struggle against ugliness. An Athenian's life is described, not untruly, as a continual, rejoicing, unreflective embrace of beauty. Uglinesses he had, and absurdities, and his eye was quick to note them. Aristophanes' sketch of the fat man in the torch-races, blown and incapable, may perhaps be remembered by some of us; with many others (as the Poet, the Sycophant, and the messenger Gods in the comedy of the Birds). But every citizen of Athens lived continually out-of-doors—" for ever delicately marching through transparent liquid air "—in the finest atmosphere on earth. He saw Hymettus and Pentelicus, and Ægina and Salamis in distance; though it is true he considered Ægina " an eye-sore." He saw Athene and Theseus, the forms of his gods and heroes, all round him; and he saw daily the living frames of strength and beauty from which the great statues were conceived. The Greek was his own model and type; he idealized man because he really knew the beauty of man. He thought the beginning and end of Art was to set forth or represent his gods and himself, which was well; and he thought his gods must be just like himself, which was not so well. He surrounded himself and his heroes with beauty, subject and auxiliary to his own beauty, exactly as the Goth carved flowers round the niches which held the statues of his saints. He studied animals, the horse in particular, as his companions (I cannot attach much importance to Myron's celebrated cow); considering himself the fairest of all animals. Accordingly, he seized on animal character with success when he tried.

Greece, as Mr. Maurice said long ago, and as every one says now, represents to us the power of the Man, of the human soul unconscious of the Divine teaching which is yet with him, not taught to look beyond himself, and contented with the glorious things within his reach; and poetry and plastic art were the most glorious of these things. His Art, then, was the natural expression of an excusable self-admiration or self-respect. Respect means looking to or looking at : the Greek honestly thought himself fit to be looked at, and he was so; and he rightly thought himself and his wife, at their best, the most beautiful objects in nature ; and he looked at, and represented himself and her accordingly; and in as far as he represented anything else, he did it in its relations to himself and wife. Let this expression pass ; it does not suit my purpose now to go into the half-Oriental relations of the sexes in Athens in the age of Phidias; let the words mean only that female beauty was rightly appreciated by Athenians, whom we must take as our representative Greeks. Goths and Northmen have felt it more strongly, partly from the honour paid to the Mother of our Lord, mainly because the effort of Christian art to look for spirituality in the face, and strive after expression, has directed attention to soft and expressive features as much as to broad chests and tough sinews. I am not going into the second or Praxitelean school of Greek art; or into its rapid decadence. In Art we love not decadence; but its first sign in Greek art, and all other, is either sensuality, or the substitution of works of conscious knowledge and methodical skill for works of inspiration. By talking of Greek works of inspiration, I mean to express my thought that the excellent spirit of the artificer was inspired, or breathed into Phidias (in particular) by the Father of Spirits; and on this subject the first few verses of Exodus xxxi. should be carefully read, and compared with the expressions of St. Paul, 1 Cor. xii. 4-6, and of St. James, i. 17. I think that while the spiritual gift is continued to the workman, while it is still given him to "see within his head" new truth or beauty, or to see old truth or beauty in a way of his own, so long art is progressive, and cannot decay. In other words, which express virtually the same thing, "When art is practised for delight, it advances: when for display, it wanes."

But now, it is all very well to say this, but can the difference between inspiration, spirituality, &c., and mere skill and learning, be proved, or seen in producible works, and can we manage to see it? I think it is possible. Let us try. Three photographs from the original work are universally accessible. The earliest one is by Phidias, and is called Theseus.* The next may be of the Augustan age, but is perhaps as late as that of Titus ; it is by Agesander of Rhodes. The third is from the Sistine, a photograph, not of a statue, but of the fresco of a statue, by Michael Angelo, and near it is his Delphic Sibyl. A fourth is the tomb of Giuliano de Medici mistaken for his brother Lorenzo, and named the Duke Lorenzo. The passage describing him in Rogers's Italy is well known to most of us.† Now, I say that there are three degrees of inspiration, or ideality, or spirituality, in these works, and that they correspond to the spiritual gift and spiritual-mindedness of their three authors. Here is the thought or spirit of Michael Angelo, servant of Christ the Lord. Here is the ideal or spirit of Phidias, seeker after God, according to his lights. Here is the skill of Agesander, seeking his own glory according to his own powers, and probably

---

* The following large photographs were hung up :

PHIDIAS.	AGESANDER.	MICHAEL ANGELO.
Theseus.	Laocoon.	Delphic Sibyl.
Ceres and Proserpine.		Male figure from Sistine.
(Ceres and Proserpine were introduced because one is a correlative in position to Theseus, and both show grandeur of draped form.)		Tomb of Duke Lorenzo, with Day and Night.

† See note at end.

to a passage in Virgil. There is spirit in the other works in different degrees; in this of his there is none. The seeking, longing faces in Michael Angelo, unsatisfied and conscious of corruption, are of course a great point of contrast between him and Phidias. But one of these fresco-pictures (not actual statues) is very like the Theseus fore-shortened; and it and the Theseus approach each other in ideality or spirituality. They are something more than highly ingenious and skilful problems in muscle, and I do not think the Laocoon is much more. That is chosen as a work of consummate skill and successful working out of the idea of a coarser and less spiritual mind; or of Virgil's description at second-hand. Let Michael Angelo wait. And in speaking of these other great works, we must not forget that Greeks really had souls and spirits, and a Father of their spirits. They were not a divine sort of Lazzaroni, nor yet a set of beautiful supernatural beings who never wore any clothes, or looked at all foolish, or did anything disgraceful. They were in great part as we are, spirits dwelling in houses of fair clay, fallen and glorious, brilliant and ruined, having vague hope in death as in life, yet infinitely less able to realize it or give reason for it than we are. Yet they had undoubtedly the great capacity, or tendency, or right which distinguishes man from brute; they had the power of prayer, of seeking right and hope from the Invisible. It is the crucial difference; and the Laureate sketches it with force and precision, as is his custom.

> For what are men better than sheep and goats
> That nourish a blind life within the brain,
> If, owning God, they lift not hands of prayer?

This is the difference between the life that is in a beast and the soul that is in a man—that the latter is capable of infinitely greater hope and aspiration beyond himself, for help, for good, for Infinite Good, for some Person to give him all of them. And this work was done in vague general service of his Gods by Phidias; he did it, not exactly because he meant to pray to Theseus, but because Theseus was a fit person to stand or sit in honour before Athene; and Athene was a manifestation or personified attribute of Zeus the one God; whom, like other thoughtful and good Greeks, he really believed on, behind all the Pantheon. I believe with Professor Zeller, in a Greek monotheism behind their polytheism. I shall appeal directly to St. Paul on that point; it does seem likely, that the better sort of Greeks, those who lived the best lives and most desired the right, worshipped Athene or Apollo as attributes of the one God of right, in the time of Pericles and Phidias. This was the spirituality of Greek art, if it had any. Being linked with idolatry, or worship of the image which is nothing, it could not last long, and men fell away from it: the second school of Attic sculpture went after Aphrodite Pandemos; and Praxiteles compounded Laises and Thaises into the form of a goddess of their profession. That is what many young gentlemen call Hellenism now. But in better days, these earlier images were worshipped as symbols manifesting features of the Unknown God: and the times of such ignorance, said St. Paul, God winked at.

Before we go to the Apostle's testimony at Lystra and Athens (and how changed and degraded an Athens) let us just run over the points of these two statues. Theseus is Phidias's simple ideal of Greek manhood in glory. He looks like the great broad-shouldered genial individual of the period: he is all strength and repose, profoundly quiet and unaffected; and has almost forgot his strength awhile, having rest, and enough to do to feel his power, without pain of fatigue. He is not what you call thoughtful; he values himself highly, but unconsciously. He never profoundly analysed himself, or anything else, in his life. His deeds and his sorrows have been great already, but they have passed, and he is still mighty among the mighty.

He is μεγαλόψυχος, high-hearted: μεγαλόψυχος, conscious of strength, valour and beauty, rejoicing in himself without vanity. I should say his laugh was a very great laugh—not frequent. He is trained from childhood to ride and to row; in harping and rhythmic speech, in song and dance and high free bearing. He can generally know a humbug when he sees him, and ask a pithy question; he is taught to fell his enemy with his fist; and sword and spear he has dealt with all his days. He loves gardening and farming; the ancient olives, the vine-rows and the violet-bed by the well come into all his poetry. He is much attached to nightingales, also he is partial to owls. For his gods, some of them are his relatives, as far as he knows: they do him much good, sometimes some wrong; then he tells them about it in good Greek. He has an idea that beyond them and their Homeric ways, which are now-and-then ungodly, there is a rightful fate or higher Zeus, in whom is all good for him. But he has an inveterate habit of making intermediate gods in his own image; and he has no notion of purity or faith with women; and those two things will be the ruin of his children, if not of him.

Now I say this statue idealizes this sort of man, the Athenian from Marathon to Arginusæ, or thereabout. The strength and repose of the statue are so subtly expressed, because Phidias was not thinking principally of muscle. The way to see strength and repose in the statue I think, is to mark the restful elbow and shoulder, the bend of the spine, and the gently exerted thigh. That is the repose. Then look at the depth of the ribs and the play of the shoulder-blade and all along them. That is strength. Who could stand before the blow of that arm? And all is so easy, that the work possesses what is called unity or self-consistency. It is one conception done at once without apparent change or experiment. Now the Laocoon has as much anatomical knowledge; probably more, in the central figure: the boys, and especially the snakes, are generally admitted to be a failure. You see its subject and object in a moment: not so with Theseus. The motives of the two works are different—one was done for indirect worship and the honour of his gods and heroes, by a very great man: the other was done directly for the honour of his own skill, by a most skilful man. And he does show his skill all over the statue, every muscle and sinew is rightly accentuated, contracting as the agony runs through the nerves like fire and ice; an æsthetic inquisitor could not have recorded the convulsions of torture more accurately: and the statue is of great value to the student accordingly. It is masterly and academic: the other is great, and has a spirit in it. The one is a laboured imitation of Pain, with coarse appeal to the passion of horror in the beholder: it is done for sensation, and anticipates Gustave Doré. The other does not regard the beholder; it is an expression of Phidias's delight in gods and heroes, and the man whom it anticipates certainly is not yet come. It answers to our first definition of true art; man's expressed delight in God's work. It is through Phidias only, as far as I can see, that Greek glyptics have any real or inner likeness to the work of Michael Angelo, whom we here take as our representative of Gothic-Christian sculpture. The autotypes, from the Sistine should be well looked at on this matter: Michael Angelo cannot have seen the Theseus; but I think any one will see the analogy and indeed resemblance, between it and this figure.

My own reading on this part of my subject has been far too fragmentary, but the names of a few cheap and very accessible books may be mentioned here, which bear on Greek art and mythology, and their connexion. Take Preller's *Greek Mythology*, and Seeman's *Gods and Heroes*. Read with these the first volume, or first two or three chapters of Max Müller's *Chips from a German Workshop*. Read also the chapters on Greek Landscape, in vol. iii. of *Modern Painters;* and there is an article, or translation of an essay by Professor Zeller, of Gottingen, on Monotheism among the Greeks, in vol. iv., p. 361, of the *Contemporary Review,* which, I believe, I have Professor Müller's authority for recommending, as I do most strongly. Lessing's *Laocoon* is a most interesting set of studies. It hardly seems necessary in talking of the Laocoon, to go into the question whether he ought to roar, or how much he ought to roar. Very loud, I should say, if at all. Homer, Virgil, and Sophocles quite agree about it, and make Mars and Hercules vocal in the extreme; also Charles Dickens. "Did I groan loud, Wackford," said Mr. Squeers, "or did I groan soft?" "Loud!" answered Wackford. Tragedy, the argument or theme of ancient tragedy, is, doubtless, the representation of man overpowered by circumstance. But whether there is not a better way of representing him thus in sculpture, than carving him with his mouth wide open, I think is a question which might be discussed. In the particular instance, I think Laocoon's roar is a sort of lion-like protest against the unjust gods, who will have an end of sacred Troy and strong-speared Priam's people. The Greeks were sensitive children of nature, and were nowise ashamed to sing out when they were hurt. If I were to make a conjecture why Gothic honour lays such stress on silent endurance of pain, I should say that it is for two reasons; first, from that vast estimation of the power and value of patience, which the Gothic world derived from Christianity; from the thought that it becomes man or woman to bear witness, to the end, that their Master forsakes them not entirely. Secondly, the hard and defiant mourir-muet principle is inherited from the Scandinavian races, stern to inflict, and stubborn to endure, who smiled or laughed in death, like Regner Lodbrog among the snakes. As a Gothic or Norsk virtue, endurance is the privilege of the strong; as a Christian virtue, it is within the reach of the weak, and of all.

Now observe, once more, the distinction between Greek Art and Gothic-Christian is that of bodily expression and spiritual expression. The Greek dwells contentedly on the bodily beauty; the Christian has been taught conviction of his own spiritual nature, and he always tries to represent or indicate it. The Greek work is more perfect, yet most of us would prefer the imperfection of the Goth—the more particularly as we cannot bridge over 2,000 years, or go back to the nature, circumstances, and surroundings which gave the Greek his powers. The visible body of man in its ideal perfection can be represented: the viewless spirit in its mystery is unable to express itself, and knows not that which it shall be. Phidias gives you one, Michael Angelo strives before you with the other. Consequently in all Christian sculpture the face is the most interesting part, dwelt on passionately by the workman. But I think this distinction is hardly enough insisted on between Phidias, and later Greek workmen, that his work was in a sense sacred, and that he probably thought he was doing service to his Gods while he carved their marble forms. And this involves the question, how far and in what sense Phidias believed in his Gods. Natural religion, or rather theogony begins with personifying the powers of nature. You have the analysis or description of the process in Müller. Greek religion goes on to personify the powers or virtues of man as attributes of God. The Aryan herdsman sees God in clouds and hears Him in the wind; the Greek will see Him in marble like himself. The former thinks that everything he sees done is done by somebody, therefore, the sunrising and sunset, the rain, and fruitful seasons, the blessings and the terrors of Nature, are done by somebody. Gradually he expresses that Personal Doer, Creator, Lord, and Father, by spoken name and visible symbol. That in few words is the progress of natural theism, with or without the help of primal tradition of revelation. So far, says St. Paul, God taught heathen to feel after Him. He left not Himself without witness, in that He did good and gave rain from heaven, and fruitful seasons, filling our hearts with food and gladness — that is St. Paul's appeal in the Spirit of God to those who would have adored Him as Mercurius. God that made the world, he tells fallen Athens, made of one blood all nations of men, that they should seek the Lord, if haply they might feel after Him and find Him (though He be not far from every one of us). In all the agony of apostolic protest against the idol and the graven image, his whole soul penetrated with the Hebrew Revelation, that the Lord our God is One God—the apostle still goes back with his hearers to the natural monotheism of their fathers, to bring them at length to God in Christ. But who of all men brought in the idol, and set up the human form for worship? The Greek above all others. You will see, the Apostle recognizes natural religion as the voice of God in man, even while his spirit is stirred within him at seeing the whole city given to idolatry. And what brought it to such idolatry? It was the great Greek spirit of personification—the Greek's way of seeing all things in himself, joined to his unprecedented sense of beauty; this made him the mightiest idolator, or maker of gods in his own image, that ever lived since God made man in His image. It seems to be this strange inversion which makes the *sin* of idolatry; that the clay should know for itself all about the potter, and contentedly make of itself to itself a sufficient representative of Him. The root of idolatry in races which do not possess revelation seems to be man's specially Greek tendency, to set himself up as an anthropomorphic sign of Deity (statue or *signum*, as the Romans called it) rather than accept the signs already given, the rain and harvest, and sunset and sunrise, and the instinct of prayer, and the love that is between man and woman, or man and man. It had been done before in symbolic nature-worship, as in Egypt. Cæsarism, or the worship of the despot, had shown itself in the days of Nebuchadnezzar if not of Nimrod. But never had man before produced images of his own beauty, which seemed so like the glory of the unseen Powers. God had made man in His own image, now man made himself an image of God. Now, of this idolatry of Athens, against which St. Paul protested, Phidias was, in one sense and age, the centre and soul, because he represents whatever good there was in it in his time. It was error and ignorance. "Yet," said St. Paul, "times of this ignorance, (your ignorance and your fathers', O Athenians!) God winked at; but now commandeth all men everywhere to repent, because he hath appointed a day, in which He will judge by that man whom He hath ordained."

But what did Phidias believe? What did other leading minds of his day believe? Consider how near he lived to the half, or whole beliefs of the mythologic age. Herodotus told all Greece at Olympia, in the most unquestioning language, how the hostile shadow had passed through the thick of strife at Marathon, felling Athenians dead and striking them blind, all covered with his streaming beard; some great ghost of days gone by, taking delight of battle as of old. He told all Greece how Phœbus Apollo was sufficient for his own, and defended his own at Delphi: he told them of the triumph of Demeter and her son rolling in its cloud across the Thriasian plain, and "brooding over the masts of Salamis," and the wrath of the landless ones, Greek Gueux de Mer, who should have revelled from Athens to Eleusis on that day; he told them of the woman's form in mid-air above the fleet at the onset, shrieking scorn on the cowards who were yet backing water, when Ameinias of Athens was on board the first Persian trireme. Ameinias was the younger brother of Æschylus, and Æschylus in all probability fought at both Marathon and Salamis: and Herodotus appeals to the testimony of men of his own time about all these wonders. To us it is a grand garland of fancies, and we believe that the men thought they saw what they said they saw. But what did Pericles and Anaxagoras, and Phidias, think about it all? What did Pericles think of Homer? Unfortunately he was so far unlike the present Prime Minister that he did not publish his views on the subject. How very interesting the comparison would be if he had. Great resemblances exist between the two statesmen; and not the least curious one is that persecution or annoyance has continually assailed them both on account of their religious views. One can quite fancy the sort of reports and questions with which Pericles may have been assailed in the Pnyx. Doubtless, with Anaxagoras at his side, Pericles would take a dubious view of Homer; but, as has been said, and as Professor Zeller ably makes out, the thoughtful Greek who really desired to find a God of Right and Justice, had an appeal in his own thoughts beyond the Homeric Zeus, to the gradually-personified Fate, the true Father of all gods and men. No thoughtful man could think that the Homeric Zeus meant anybody in Pericles' day. But Pericles and the leading minds of Athens did not go one whit nearer atheism, because they saw there must be some mistake about the Homeric Zeus: they simply went back to a higher unknown Zeus, who was really just and all-ruling, and lord of himself as well as of other things. And the higher they placed him, in infinity of goodness and infinity of power, the more monotheism prevailed over polytheism in their minds. If Zeus be an unknown Zeus of all Right and Good, thought the better Greek, then there is One Person to ask for Right and Good. He lives somewhere, under some conditions. Why should not we, if we do the right, go to Him and be as He is? Why should not those who are with Him and please Him, come back to us, *i. e.* within reach of our senses?

Why not, indeed? So probably thought Pericles and Anaxagoras, and Herodotus and Æschylus, and Phidias and the men of Marathon. I do not speak of professional traders in doubt or denial, sophists in the bad sense; we can all form a tolerable notion of what they are like, as the breed is by no means extinct. But these men believed in Spirit, and in their own spirit, and in a Father of Spirits. For myths or adumbrations of Him, they took them silently: prayer and sacrifice seemed good to them, and established ritual would do for them. They thought of the myths of heroes as Alva may have thought of Roman Catholic legend; or Cortes of the appearance of Santiago; or Cato of the Dioscuri at Regillus.

Then as to the great athletic statues, we may take Myron's *Discoboli* as good specimens of what they were like. Nobody can respect the late Professor of Poetry in Oxford more than I do; but it is extraordinary to me that, with all his Hellenism, Mr. Arnold says so little of Greek art. No man knows more of the ideas of the contemporaries of Phidias; no man says less of Phidias himself; while the great Documents, the original hand-writing of Phidias, are within one hundred and fifty yards of every one who enters the Library of the British Museum. How far would he not go to see the undoubted MSS., autograph and holograph, of Ædipus Tyrannus or Colonæus, in Sophocles' hand? Yet we have no evidence of his ever having looked at the work of Phidias' hand, which Sophocles looked at and enjoyed every day of his life. London is very unlike Athens; but those who want to see or study Greek Art need not think of going out of London. It is said that while Greek athletics made Greece the delight and honour of the world, ours only disgust and offend all nations except ourselves. But why did Greek gymnastics or athletics delight all mankind? Because of the art, the sculpture which immortalized the beauty of the athlete: because the statues commemorate the great games, or services of reverent delight to the personified powers of nature; because in Greece athletics and art went together, and went the right way too; as service to God, according to men's light. To go on about Greece and Hellenism, without appreciating the extent to which every Greek was trained by the eye, is to leave out of account a great part of Greek education; which, as I say, differed from ours in this, that we analyze beauty without seeing it, and they saw it without analysis. For beauty of form, I do not think the Greeks had finer specimens of it than the higher Gothic races. A great Roman revival of sculpture came from Græcised study of Gothic forms. The Germanicus looks like an instance of this, though it must, I suppose, be assigned to the younger Cleomenes (about B.C. 200). I certainly prefer it to the Apollo, or even the Antinous, personally speaking: it seems to me both ideal and academic. And, to speak one word for ourselves, I doubt whether eight mightier men, or better models, were ever produced at Olympia, than the four English and four American lads who rowed the Harvard race. The broad assertion, that the Gothic form is not equal to the Greek in beauty, is founded on conventional standards of beauty, based on measurements from Greek statues. In an excellent work, Dr. Fau's *Anatomy*, this astounding addition is made to it: that the forms of children, male or female, possess no beauty at all. Beauty must be used here in some stricter sense, in which we are not using it. But here is one more photograph, easy to obtain, and not of a Greek statue. Did you ever see anything more like Apollo? The square broad brow, the hair, the pride of the bow-shaped lips, the eyes severely bright, the round chin, and long hard neck. Many will know who it is. It is Tom King who beat Heenan. Tom King, now a preacher, declaring such faith as is in him to all men, believing himself to be called to that work.

Professor Arnold in one of his works makes an allusion, well worthy of our attention, to the opposition between Christian asceticism and Hellenic happiness. The consciousness of sin, and the Lord's death for sin, he says, in the words of George Herbert, "banished joy" from the soul. There is no doubt that asceticism has had great influence on Christian art, or that it is logically traceable to the doctrine of sin and corruption. But actual and practical asceticism among Greek Christians began because of actual corruption in the Hellenic world. It is a question whether the Greek world of the second century had much joy in the life it lived or the vices it practised. But if it had, undoubtedly Christianity did banish a great deal of such joy. Were Greeks much happier, really, for not knowing that they were rather corrupt? If so, the faith interfered with that sort of happiness.

And no doubt, asceticism has borne hard on art. I do not care to distinguish the severity of the early Church from that of Puritanism or Protestantism. Both began alike, with the search of purity of spirit in an evil time, and necessary separation from the world, and consequent persecution—and both, after being the rule of many noble and innocent lives, became a burden no man·could bear. But as to Christianity setting itself against art, the Christians made all the use they could, of the art-work of heathen and Christian hands alike, in the Catacombs. Every symbol and myth and decoration which was not absolutely contrary to and directed against the faith, Christians cheerfully accepted. The popular contrast between Greek beauty and Christian barbarism is pleasingly brought out in a plaintive passage in Thackeray somewhere—*The Newcomes*, I think—

where he follows Gibbon, who followed Libanius, who followed the philosophic wailings of his day; and idealizes the brutal Christian mob breaking into the temples, and smashing the fair, calm faces of the marble gods, and so on. Mr. Thackeray did not mean it; but Gibbon and Libanius meant to imply that it was the Christian faith which had made the mob brutal. St. Paul had taken away their natural taste for beauty. I wonder how much they really had to take away about his time. Demetrius of Ephesus did not say much about beauty, as a practical man, afraid of loss in his business. There is some difference between the Greece of Pericles and that of Ptolemy. Were the crowds of Rome, Corinth, or Alexandria so very æsthetic, or pure, or tranquil, before St. Paul; or did he and his corrupt their artistic feeling? Had these same rough iconoclasts any particular reason to love the fair calm faces of the pagan gods? What had those gods or their friends done for the brutal Christian crowd? The believers in the fair calm gods had had Christians continually broiled alive in their honour; the fair calm faces had been lustrated with the smoke of torment, and never looked one whit less calm. And the philosophers, who did not the least believe in the fair calm gods, had looked on at ease while the faces of Christian women were smashed by tigers or wild bulls. I am at a loss to see why maimed martyrs, like St. Paphnutius, for instance, should have been expected to address themselves to the artistic sympathies of Constantine in the names of Scopas and Praxiteles. You all know that most striking passage in the Dean of Westminster's account of the Council of Nice. When the council met, a strange grim figure halted up to meet the Emperor, having one thigh withered to the hip with cutting and branding, and one eye thrust out, and being otherwise horribly disfigured. It was Paphnutius of the Upper Thebaid; and it was noticed how the great Lord of the world took the old man in his arms, and set his lips tenderly to the eyeless socket, which had last looked on the light of fire and steel, to be endured to extremity in the fore-front of the battle of the Lord. When Constantine kissed Paphnutius, no doubt he kissed an unhellenic and inartistic-looking person. But it could hardly be expected that that person would care much for the Apollo Belvedere. And I don't care for him either—for his long legs, or his chignon, or the attempt at facial expression, which may be scornful, or may be only *stuck-up*. Now, this same Paphnutius, martyr in both will and deed, he bore the strongest testimony in the Council of Nice, ἐβόᾳ μάκρα at the top of his voice (grotesquely and unhellenically, of course) against the very central injunction of asceticism—that is to say, against clerical and lay celibacy in general. He vehemently refused to impose on others, as a yoke, the burden he willingly bore himself. It is quite clear that ascetics of this character were not men who would reject fresco or mosaic as means of Christian teaching; nor did any convent of ascetics ever do so that I know of. Christianity would have done art no good by encouraging it to multiply Laocoons and Aphrodites, had that been possible. But Christian people, as we see from *Bottari, De Rossi,* and all works on the Catacombs, did undoubtedly encourage and make use of the expiring energies of Græco-Roman art. Next time I shall be able to show you tracings illustrative of the transition of the earliest classical work of the Catacombs into the earliest style of purely Christian art—that is to say, the Byzantinism of Ravenna. Up to the sack by Alaric, Rome is the seat of Græco-Christian art, which degenerates and barbarizes with all other art, until, with Alaric's taking of Rome, "at one stride comes the dark;" and the art of the Catacombs ceases. Save its changed relics in Ravenna and Byzantium, Greek art dies in the Catacombs, till the Lombard revival. We cannot have more than a very short summary, of facts mostly controverted, about these Christian sepulchres; but we shall often have to refer to them. As in other things, I believe I know something of the matter; but that is nothing to the quantity I do not know.

First, as to the authenticity of these paintings; that is to say, as to whether they are of the same date as the walls they are painted on. I take the paintings first. You will see in Bottari's work, that some of the sepulchral Christian bas-reliefs are, happily, dated: the earliest he gives is that of Junius Bassus, A.D. 358, and very beautiful it is. The Commendatore de Rossi is, of course, inclined to plead for the highest degree of antiquity for everything, and Mr. Northcote's book follows him. Mr. J. H. Parker is at the opposite pole of opinion, and he is inclined to refer a large majority of these works, in the cemetery of S. Callixtus and elsewhere, to that great beginning of Christian decoration, which originated in the time, and by the enthusiasm, of St. Paulinus[*] of Nola. And he is enabled by the unmistakeable resemblance of frescoes in the Catacombs to dated mosaics, to conclude that many works described as of the second

---

[*] Born 353, died 431. Pupil of St. Ambrose.

and third centuries are really of the fifth and sixth, and I must agree with him. Nevertheless, he makes exception in favour of various paintings of the Fish and the Good Shepherd; and I think probably of the Vine and other symbols taken from Holy Scripture. It is well to take the absolutely unbiassed testimony of Dr. Theodore Mömmsen.* He begins by explaining that as Jewish Catacombs of the highest antiquity exist to this day; and as burial was a Pagan custom as well as burning, the Catacombs are not exclusively Christian. He throws doubt on, or he is not satisfied with, the derivation of the word from κατα and *cumbo* or τύμβος, or the Spanish *catar* to see, etc. But he specifies two sets of paintings as examples; one in the Callixtine Catacomb, the other, on which he lays special stress, in the sepulchre called of Flavia Domitilla, granddaughter of Vespasian;† who is known to have been exiled for the faith, after the martyrdom of her husband. These he describes, and they would be of the greatest antiquity. And in these the dying Græco-Roman Art survives—as in Pompeii and the cities of Magna Græcia. This is quite unlike Ravenna. Anybody can see the freedom and beauty of the vine-branches here, with the boy-

---

* *Contemporary Review*, May, 1871.
† Near the Church of SS. Nereus and Achilles.

vintagers. Well, this is (No. 1, page 66) nearest in treatment and design to the well-known later mosaic in the church of St. Constantine, at Rome, dated 320, by Mr. Parker. Professor Mömmsen is sure that this painting in Flavia Domitilla's tomb is of the date of the building.* There are similar paintings in the Callixtine Catacomb :—the figures of the Good Shepherd, the Fish bearing Bread, the history of Jonah, etc. Of the date of the tomb itself, he is not so certain. It cannot be later than Hadrian, he says; and he leaves it an open question as to its being really the foundation of a granddaughter of Vespasian—by no means denying it, but thinking the case for it incomplete. One instance is as good as any number for our purpose, and these may be taken as specimens of the earliest Christian symbolic paintings, and the last relics of Greek technical skill, used with Greek sense of beauty. Soon we come to the monk's work, and the Ostrogoth's; neither of them to be despised; but both alike beginning without a shadow of teaching in form. Earnestness of faith, desire to communicate fact and doctrine, and oriental glory of colour, now enter the ring; and their great documents are the mosaics of Ravenna.

* Before A.D. 98, if authentic.

No. 1. The Vine:
Earliest Christian Work,
Callixtine Catacomb.
Bottari ii. T. 74.

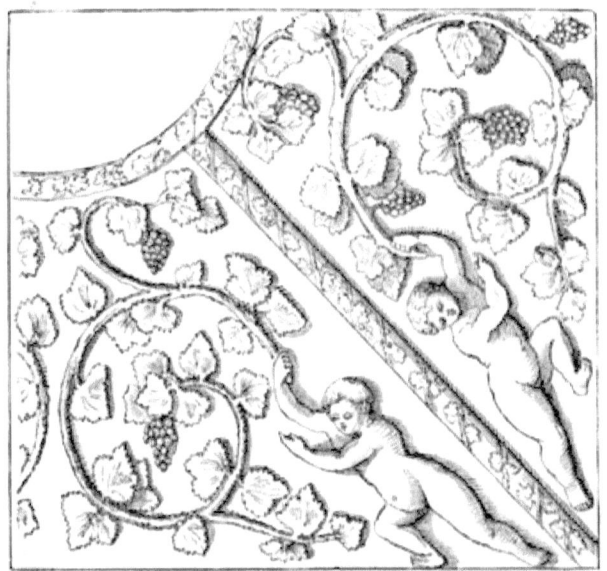

No. 2. The Vine. Transitional. From Cemetery on Latin Way. Bottari ii. tav. 93.

No. 3. Byzantine. Sixth Century. Tomb of Galla Placidia.

I began this by bringing several works of central and typical character before you : the personification of noble manhood by Phidias; the height of academic skill in the Laocöon ; and two or three works of Michael Angelo, which express transcendent spiritual power.* Then, speaking of the technical practice óf Art, I said, in effect, that Christianity inherited faint traditions of Greek Art through Rome, and in later days recovered and learnt much from great ancient models; but that the generic distinction between Greek and Christian Art survives, in the contented and perfect bodily beauty of the one, and the facial power, and effort for spiritual expression, in the other. Nevertheless, it seemed that the works of Phidias had in them the expression of such religious feeling as was possible for him ; and we were led to consider how far he and his contemporaries could see through, and beyond, their idolatry. And it seems that St. Paul appeals to a monotheism, which he knew to exist even behind the grosser Athenian idolatry of his own day, and which earlier Greeks must have held also. Then we spoke of Christian asceticism, or severe treatment of the body to which the Greek gave such abundant honour; and I protested against the idea that the Christians had any particular objection to

* Note in Appendix on Sculpture of the Sacristy of S. Lorenzo.

Art and beauty in the martyr ages; only pointing out that they were hardly to be expected to care for sculpture which was fully identified with the system which was always flogging and burning them. We then began to consider, how willingly they made use of the relics of Greek beauty in the decorations of the Catacombs. In these earliest works Greek and Christian Art meet, the one in its senility, the other in helpless infancy. In the great Renaissance of the fifteenth century, Greek Art came back to the Teutonic world, as an adjunct to Greek literature, with great results. But before that, there had been repeated Renaissances of Art, north and south of the Alps: not Greek, but Lombard, French, Florentine, Saxon and Norman-English. One or two of these we shall consider in these lectures.

LECTURE III.

ITALIAN ART-HISTORY.

I SAID we had followed Græco-Roman art to its grave, last lecture; for it was buried in the Catacombs, with many things: with bones of martyrs and confessors; with strange scattered relics of Gentile life; with the remains of an ancient world and system dead and buried out of sight; with the histories and memories of 350 miles of human sepulchres. Here it rested for awhile, and hence the old lessons of Christian symbolism rose again, and have been used ever since for the picture-preaching of the Faith. Let me run over a few facts about the Catacombs to you. There are about sixty-five on all sides of Rome: their aggregate length, as I said, may be estimated at 350 miles. They are worked in the soft tufa rock,—volcanic mud, cooled and hardened; and in that only — avoiding marshy or low ground, and also the harder puzzolana or building-stone. It is not true, says Professor Mömmsen, that they originated in the numberless sand and puzzolana pits round Rome. Their arrangements are quite inconsistent with this: the narrow passages, three-quarters or half a metre in breadth, and intersecting at right angles, cannot be quarried-out space for getting stone, and there are no wide passages or roads for leading it when got. "These vaults have been devised for one object only, to get as much wall as possible in a given space, of such depth as to admit of tombs on each side. In some instances the real sand, or stone pits, have been found within the Catacombs, very differently arranged, with broad passages and conveniences for carrying the sand to the surface; but these pits are evidently more ancient, and either shut off altogether by the builders of the catacomb, or utilised for their purpose by intermediate walls. The enormous space occupied by the burial vaults of Christian Rome, in their extent not surpassed even by the system of cloacæ or sewers of Republican Rome, is certainly the work of that community which St. Paul addressed in his Epistle to the Romans—a living witness of its immense development."

There is no doubt then that the Catacombs may be said to be mainly and originally Christian, though not exclusively so. The earlier Jewish Catacombs, marked by the seven-branch candlestick on the walls, are of course an exception. But the use of burial as against burning distinguishes, in a general way, Christian treatment of the dead from heathen. The Christians always buried, the heathen generally burned. Burial was a heathen custom also; and after a body had been burnt one bone at least of it was to be buried, by Roman pontifical law. Still burning was *the* heathen custom, and with the middle classes the light "compact"* ashes were kept in jars and ranged on shelves in pigeon-holes made in the sides of pits, called Columbaria or pigeon-cotes. Now, in the very earliest Christian times everybody who had a piece of ground seems to have been buried in it. There a mausoleum, or chapel, or cella memoriæ was built, if he had been a rich or well-known man— heathen or Christian, and there his family and friends assembled from time to time for memorial feasts. Thus, Professor Mömmsen thinks, arose the first Christian churches and chapels before Constantine's time. And there can be no doubt that agapæ, or love-feasts, whether completed or not completed by the Eucharistic celebration, took place here also. They form a difficult subject which is not for us now.

* εὐθέτου σποδοῦ, Æschylus, Agamemnon, 443, Dind.

The point is, that Christians soon came to desire to be buried together as Christians; to be, in death, assemblages of the church, as they had been living congregations on earth,* and therefore they excluded heathens from burial with them.

For a visit to, say the Calixtine Catacomb, you go out on the Appian Way; by the road on which Horace left Rome for Brundusium, and St. Paul approached Rome from Puteoli; you turn off into somebody's vineyard, not very far from the round tower of Cæcilia Metella; a bundle of thin tapers are produced and lighted, and you go down a flight of narrow steep steps, two, three, or four flights; for there are as many as four stories in these houses of death. Where the first range of tombs may begin will depend on the thickness of sand and soil above the tufa rock. Then you are in a narrow gallery between rows of stone niches, graves mostly despoiled, all in soft drab-coloured rock, plastered and painted here and there. They are wonderfully like berths in a cabin, only the sleep obtained in them is so much more sound. The single graves are called loculi; the larger ones, where the rock is hollowed into an apse, or half cupola, above a sarcophagus, are arcosolia. Cubicula are square chambers surrounded with tombs, and were no doubt places of worship; the Eucharist being generally celebrated on the grave of a martyr. Here then on these walls the skill of Christian painters, sometimes of Gentiles, was employed to decorate them with the symbols of the faith.

But our subject for to-day is early Italian art history.

There may appear at first sight to be two strong objections to the attempt to trace any connexion or succession in schools of painting and sculpture, from the earliest Græco-Christian work in the Roman Catacombs to these days of English landscape painting. First, it is impossible to do it within the compass of an essay; secondly, it may seem impossible to do it at all. But we spoke of Art, in the first instance, as an expression of man's delight in God's work, which he calls nature; and naturalism and reality are a sufficient connexion between schools of living Art in all ages. So many men have come and seen, and rejoiced, and recorded their delight in nature. Their Art has often been symbolic as well as literal or historical; representing things not actually existing. But symbolism is capable of naturalist treatment. Assyrian bulls, or Egyptian sphinxes, or Gothic griffins, are good Art based on nature, if their authors had enough of the spiritual gift of imagination to fuse into one object the natural characteristics of two or three animals. The Assyrian symbol has the strength of the bull, the wings of the eagle, and the human face of command, truly rendered as seen: the Lombard griffins have their compound nature of lion and eagle faithfully characterized: the workman saw within his head, by memory from nature and his own power of conception, that which he meant to carve, before he touched hammer or chisel.

This naturalism, or intense perception of, and delight in representing, the visible work of God, is the common feature of early-Christian, Gothic, or modern Art. It may be said to dawn in the Catacombs, and a few carvings at Ravenna, and rise above the horizon in the ancient churches of Pavia, or Lucca, or Verona, or St. Ambrogio at Milan. Perhaps the best example we can have is the front of St. Zenone at Verona, with its bronze gates anticipating Ghiberti, and repeating the ancient scriptural symbolisms of the Catacombs,[*] along with historical subjects. With these there are huntings, and fightings, and grotesques; the Gothic fancy is in its full strength here: but in these gates and on this front, the early naturalism of Gothic work is

---

[*] See p. 128: "The Lombard Noah."

connected with the last Græco-Roman efforts at representation of nature. Greek or Græco-Roman Art dies in the Catacombs; Dr. Theodore Mömmsen says that they were closed, as cemeteries, after the taking of Rome by Alaric, in 410; though they may have been afterwards adorned, painted, and repainted as places of pilgrimage. But the early sepulchral Art clings to nature, and symbolism direct from nature, aiming at the character of natural objects. Its vines are from nature; its sheep are made as like sheep as the painter or mosaicist can manage; its doves are just like real doves, and its palm-trees like palms. Even the later Byzantinism retained reference to nature, and truth in conventional work.* Moreover, it seems clear from passages from De Rossi, that the Christian artists of the later empire were like the Gothic Christians in this other great respect; that they desired to bring all things into church; to represent all their ways and thoughts in their sacred places. Of course peaceful and weak men did this in a different way from warlike and strong men. The Veronese churches show us how the Lombard Goths did their work. Let us take De Rossi's account, and see how secular things, and crafts, and pursuits are represented by Græco-Roman Christians

* *Stones of Venice*, vol. iii. plate iv. The Byzantine Olive.

in the Catacombs, as in Gothic churches. "It is a fact I have constantly observed," he says, "in the subterranean cemeteries, that Christians of the earliest times made use of sarcophagi, without any special Christian symbols upon them, and probably the work of heathen hands, containing images of the stars and seasons, and scenes of pastoral life and agriculture, some even of the chase, and some of a comic character. The Christians gave their own sense to scenes of husbandry and shepherd life, personifications of the seasons, dolphins, and sea-monsters. Anything which was free from idolatrous imagery, or did not actually represent Pagan deities, they freely made use of." And he goes on with curious illustrations of the Christian desire to find foreshadowings of the history of their own faith in ancient legend. We all know how Orpheus, in particular, is used in the Callixtine and other catacombs as a symbol of our Lord. So also with representations of Hercules, Deucalion, and others. The Christian symbolist, or parabolic artist, had no more hesitation in using a heathen myth to impress a fact of Christian history, than he had in using Pagan paint or Pagan brushes to record it on the cemetery wall.

The subject of Christian symbolism requires a

paper to itself, which will contain some notes of how spiritual teaching—all centering in the ideas, or thought, or faith—call it which you will—of the Incarnation and of the Cross—has gone on from the first days till now; how it has been parabolic or symbolic; and how its symbolism has been represented in fresco, in bas-relief, in mosaic; by illuminations in books for those who could afford them, by church paintings and windows, and by acted pictures or mysteries, for those who could not. For the present I have to go on with the history of carved or pictured beauty, and observe where the Goths or Teuton races inherited faint traditions of it.

Theodoric the Ostrogoth, Dietrich of Bern or Verona, the historical vanquisher of Odovakar or Odoacer, the mythical champion of the great Rabenschlacht or Battle of Ravenna, belongs to Gibbon's *Decline and Fall;* and also to the *Nibelungenlied*. He is one of those mighty and rough-hewn personages of history who loom in grandeur half-made-out, like the head and shoulders of Michael Angelo's statue of Day. So is Frederick Barbarossa; so in part are Charlemagne and Cœur-de-Lion, so are the fainter shades of Arthur and Odin; so, to all the Mahommedan world, is Solomon, son of David. Well, this Dietrich, or Theodoric, hero of primitive

Byzantine Capital, Ravenna

romance, perfectly real and practical maker of modern history and builder of Ravennese temples, had his cipher carved on one of these capitals, which now stand in great beauty where he set them, in the market-place of Ravenna. That he was sent to Constantinople at eight years of age as a hostage in 463, (ten years after the voice had come by night to the anxious Emperor, crying that the bow of Attila was broken);—that he was there trained worthily for war and administration; that he was, on the whole, faithful to the Emperors Leo and Zeno, though he had at last to march on Constantinople; that Zeno diverted his forces to Italy; that he conquered Odovakar in 490; that for thirty-three years he strove to do judgment and justice, to an extent to which Italy and the world were totally unaccustomed; that though a half-convert or Arian only, he encouraged the orthodox faith; that he long honoured and cared for Boethius and Symmachus, and at last slew them in the jealousy of his old age, and died heart-broken with remorse, and partly of terror in recognizing the Roman profile of Boethius, at dinner, in a large cod's head and shoulders—that is common knowledge, at least as true as history in general. He lies at Ravenna, under a huge monolith, in a round tower of other days which time has hardly touched, but which is slowly sinking into the wet soil. The earth is quietly absorbing one of the mightiest of her children. But he, and his daughter Amalosuntha, seem to have delighted in Byzantine Art; and all the most interesting work in Ravenna is done by Greeks or Græco-Romans; under a new conventual phase, at the bidding and under the patronage of the Goth. In Cairo and Jerusalem too, you may see the Byzantine work done, and done with the greatest clearness, grace, and sense of beauty, by Greeks for Caliphs. Here in Ravenna it is done for Ostrogoths. Greek hands and teaching may be traced far north; in Rhenish carvings, as the Station-Crosses of Mayence, and Planig.* To follow them into Saxon and Irish illumination, is not for us now.† But Byzantinism is a very different thing from the Græco-Roman art of the Catacombs; as also from the Romanesque work of the Lombard churches, which has more in common with the naturalisms and fancies of the earliest Christians. And let us just say what we understand by some of these words, and how we distinguish their meaning.

---

* See the *Jahrbucher des Vereins von Alterthumsfreunden in Rheinlande*, p. 175. (Bonn. 1868.)
† See Professor Westwood's works.

Roman Art I have called Græco-Roman, because all its ornament and beauty of decoration is derived from Greece. It is properly called Roman, because all its constructive beauty or grandeur belongs to Rome. Rome gave us the round arch, and all round-arched building is Roman; call it Romanesque in Italy, where the influence and name of old Rome still weighed with the builder or artist; call it Byzantine, where the influence of the earlier Rome came to the builder through Byzantium, or Constantinople, or new Rome. Constantinople is called Rome to this day by Greeks, Turks, and Russians: little reck they of the White Pope, the White Priest of Italy, and his Eternal City. Well, call the Roman round arch Norman when its soffits and edges are done in zigzags; call it Moorish when the round arch becomes the waggon arch, and the cove of the Arab tent is added to it; call it Cinque-cento when it becomes mongrel, and you can't call it anything else. Round arches, at all events, are Roman, because they suited the Roman cloacæ, and vaultings, and brick architecture. The Lombard, or Saracen, or the latter first, or both of them together, pointed the arch like a lance-point, or the Norman noticed the intersections of his round arches; and he foliated it for symbolism of the Holy Trinity, and sometimes because he loved green leaves. But the Byzantine ornament is our subject now; it is chiefly in mosaic that I shall speak of it, because the Ravennese mosaics are its chief expression and best example, with those of St. John Lateran and St. Constantia at Rome. Now, we all associate Byzantine work with stiffness, and most of us know something of its want of grace in drawing the figure. The splendour of Byzantine colour is generally appreciated; and an idea may be formed from Dietrich's capital, or from the specimens given in the *Stones of Venice*, how very great beauty of drawing, of line, and light and shade, the Byzantine retained in decoration; using, most commonly, vegetable forms, or those of birds. Splendour of colour, I say, remains; with much conventional grace of form. Why does all beauty of human representation depart? You have it, or the attempt at it, in the earliest work of the Catacombs; in the vintagers, in Orantes, and other figures. Yet, you soon see that a change is passing over it: the type of outer distress and inward despondency. The ascetic, or conventual change is passing over the Christian life; and, as it advances, so surely does all the drawing on the sepulchres become stiffer, and more depressed, and gloomy. Art has fled for refuge to the cloister; and the monks' brains are reeling with controversy; storm after storm of Arianism breaks on their heads; the Goths will not see distinctions *they* must die for; kings and queens are against them; their hearts are failing them with terror for the desolation of Italy; for the sword of the Lombard is shaken against her. The dwellers in Italian convents and churches, through the age between Attila and Alboin, had to look on such evil without relief or hope of change, such distress and apparent failure of the faith as probably can only be equalled, *mutatis mutandis*, in the great centres of modern civilization. Besides, conventual severities and ascetic treatment of the human body deprived it of sacredness or beauty in the eyes of recluses. They gradually shrink from representing our Lord. His face grows more severe, because they look for Him as Judge and Avenger only—the mirror of their world is too dark for them to see His face in. The following extract from Mr. Lecky speaks of the tenth century, though the change he describes as complete, of course began earlier; and indeed, it is observable in Catacomb paintings of late date. Of Christian Art, he says: "The places decorated were the Catacombs: the chapels were all surrounded by the dead; the altar upon which the sacred mysteries were celebrated was the tomb of a martyr. It would seem but natural that the great and terrible scenes of Christian vengeance should be depicted. Yet nothing of this kind appears in the Catacombs: with two doubtful exceptions, there are no representations of martyrdom. Daniel unharmed amid the lions; the unaccomplished sacrifice of Isaac; the Three Children unscathed amid the flames; and St. Peter led to prison, are the only images that reveal the horrible persecution that was raging. There was no disposition to perpetuate forms of suffering: no ebullition of bitterness or complaint; no thirsting for vengeance. Neither the Crucifixion, nor any of the scenes of the Passion, were ever represented: nor was the Day of Judgment, nor were the sufferings of the lost. The wreaths of flowers in which Paganism delighted, and even some of the more joyous images of the Pagan mythology, were still retained, and were mingled with all the most beautiful emblems of Christian hope, and with representations of the miracles of mercy." "After the tenth century, he says, the Good Shepherd, which adorns every chapel in the Catacombs, is no more seen; the miracles of mercy are replaced by the details of the Passion, and the terrors of the Last Judgment. About the twelfth century this change becomes almost universal. From this period, writes one of the most learned of modern archæologists, Christ appears more and more melancholy, and truly terrible. It is, indeed, the Rex tremendæ majestatis of a Dies Iræ."

This is true in its main points. There *is* one Crucifix in the Catacombs, evidently of the time of Charlemagne. Some account of the Christian use of the Cross and the Crucifix will be found in the next Paper. It appears to me from observations made in Eastern Greek convents, at Mount Sinai in particular (on comparing them with early MSS.), that the severe or melancholy representation of Our Lord begins very early, and has a good deal to do with the unskilfulness of the workman. There is a transition face, as we may call it, at Ravenna in the Church of S. Apollinare Nuova, with the great eyes and heavy eyebrows which afterwards become mere caricature in the MSS. and elsewhere. This would date from Justinian; and the harsh work in his convent of the Transfiguration, at Mount Sinai, corresponds to it. Then in the Duomo at Torcello, the mother city of Venice, there is perhaps the earliest mosaic of the Last Judgment in existence. Neither the building nor its original ornaments can be of much later date than the first settlement on the Lagune islets—perhaps of those who fled from

Attila in 452, or certainly from Alboin in 568.*
The red stream of its lake of fire, and the worms
writhing in the eyeless skulls, will be remembered
by all who have seen it. There is no doubt of
the despairing severity of much Byzantine Art; but
it is the effect of Eastern asceticism; and it is
sharpened by the sense of corruption in Christian
life itself, and by external distress. It changes in
some of the Gothic schools, and almost vanishes, and
again and again recurs, like a spectre which is always
near, but visible only at noon and midnight. And
this severity must hang over Christian thought —
over all religious or spiritual thought, unto the end
—a shadow of warning, a shadow of death, even of
the second death. Not only does the world pass
away with all its shows and all its beauty, but there
shall be judgment. There remaineth a fearful looking
for, which no faith, or definite form of religion ever
denies or avoids; a human sense of justice and judgment, inevitable and irresistible. Priests really did
not fabricate that penal doctrine, which every priest
on earth, not being a madman, would certainly give
his life to be able to deny in God's name.

Once more let me try to begin about Ravenna.
The interest of the place centres for us in its ancient

* See p. 95.

mosaics, not later than the time of Justinian : we will not stop to moralize on it as the residence of Dante or of Byron. The city was once a seaport : it is a stranded Venice, situated at the southern point of the great horseshoe or Delta formed by the Po and its tributaries from Alp and Apennine. Venice is at the other extremity, and perhaps, centuries hence, will suffer the fate of Ravenna, and be divorced from the Adriatic, to which she used annually to be wedded. What was once the port wherein rode the Adriatic Fleet of Rome, from Augustus to Alaric, is now the pretty Maremma-looking village of St. Apollinaris in Classe, and the sea is only visible from its campanile. I must speak very generally of its mosaics. They are found in the Chapel of Galla Placidia, the Church of St. Vitale, St. John the Evangelist, and St. Apollinare Nuova, called Nella Citta, and the two Baptisteries. I shall read the following account of some of the art of these churches : their symbolism is reserved for the next Paper. This is directly from notes on the spot, extended and verified while my memory was fresh :—

" In comparing the primitive art of Rome with that of Ravenna, one is struck by the obvious difference between Art derived through Rome from ancient Greece, and the purely Christian work of the Adriatic city, wrought by Byzantine hands, and with Eastern splendour of colour. Beauty of form is scarcely aimed at, or is merely decorative; but the principle of symbolic art-preaching is in full force. Until these great mosaics are copied in the same material, it is to be feared that a good idea cannot be obtained of them without a journey to Ravenna. They are distinguishable from those in St. Mark's at Venice by the subordination of the gold backgrounds to the most wonderful gradations of dark azure and green in the figures and decorations, which range in colour from the hues of deep sea and purple night to those of malachite and emerald. The high lights in all of them are put in boldly and precisely with golden tesseræ, and white figures are introduced as freely as in the atrium of St. Mark's. Crimsons and scarlets are more rarely used, and made *precious* in the work, as Mr. Ruskin says. The processions of male and female saints in St. Apollinare Nuova are a delightful illustration of this; and so many distressing photographs of them are in circulation, necessarily conveying ideas of utter gloom, blackness, and barrenness to the public, that we will vainly try to describe the glorious hues which deck those forgotten walls with the after-glow of the sunken Past.

"The purple and white marble columns of the

central aisle of the basilica support on each side a processional frieze in mosaic of male and female saints, ended on the male side with the Lord in Glory, a head and face of extreme beauty, though with something of the sadness of later and fallen Art; on the female side, by an Adoration of the Magi, exactly like some in the Roman Catacombs. All the figures are white-robed, and tread on emerald-green turf, separated from each other by upright palms bearing scarlet dates.* They are shod also with scarlet, and bear small crowns in their hands lined with the same colour. The background is of gold, not bearing a large proportion to the size of the figures; but above them are white single figures with ample golden spaces; and a third course of singular representations of New Testament subjects runs round just below the roof, with backgrounds of alternate gold and black; black, or the darkest purple, also prevailing, relieved with gold, in the roof.† The splendid and jewelled effect of the whole is beyond praise, and its brilliant lightness makes it especially suitable to the dark

* The palm is used in Rome as in Ravenna: but the Eastern workmen seem always to *insist on the fruit*, which is generally omitted in Rome.

† Giotto may have derived his taste for blue backgrounds, &c., from Ravenna. Nothing can be more interesting than to compare his lovely frescoes in the northern chapel of St. Giovanni with the mosaics of the nave.

aisle of a great city. We cannot but hope that it may find favour with the restorers of our metropolitan cathedral, where processions of figures must certainly be a part of the decorations, and reflected light will necessarily be a great object.

"As has been said, the symbolisms of the Ravenna church walls are similar in subject with those of the Catacombs, consisting both of emblematic objects, as lambs or palms, and of historic or symbolic pictures of events. Birds are imitated with delightful realism in St. Vitale; but the Gothic energy is strongly repressed, as yet, by Byzantine rule and its languor; and non-symbolic or secular carvings are rarer than in the Catacombs—far more so than in the Veronese churches. The transition thither from Ravenna is the passage from Ostrogothic or semi-Byzantine Art to the untamable vigour of the Lombard fancy. It is true, that knights on horseback, running stags, ducks, a grotesque head and legs, and a mermaid, bear witness to some Teutonic sculptor in St. Giovanni Evangelista at Ravenna; and the vestry of the same church contains what appears to be a first attempt at historical mosaic (of Theodoric's siege of Constantinople, and other profane and sacred subjects)—which I take to be the most powerfully comic Art-production in all the wide world."

Observe only, in the first place, that there is no image of Pain, Pœna, Penalty of Sin, or Punishment —these words are all the same. That the artists believed in such punishment there can be no shadow of doubt; but the Church did not allow them to employ their imaginations on ghastly images of it. She did not use Art to proclaim terrors she was not allowed to deny; and as did the Catholic Church up to the end of the seventh century—so does the Anglican Church to this day. Even the Cross, at Ravenna, is always very richly and brightly ornamented, and is used as a symbol of the Person of our Lord, rather than of His sufferings. Observe, we here pass from the Art of ancient Rome—derived from Greece, and last observed in the Catacombs— to the Art of Byzantium, which preserved the relics of Greek beauty in a strange and gilded repose; or, "like a museum of fossils,"—to use the expression of a man much beloved, early dead and deeply regretted —the late Lord Lothian. Every one who has read his letters on Italian History and Art will feel a strange regret and wonder, that such powers and early performance, rather than promise, were so soon withdrawn from the world.

To turn from Byzantine colour and design to history, we go back to a time long before the Ravennese mosaics were finished. Close to the year 450, the lovely chapel of Placidia began to be built for the world-wearied Augusta. "She had lived long enough to see the billows of calamity over her sire and children borne—stroke after stroke, sea after sea,"—and here she found rest. Her embalmed corpse might still be seen till a century ago, when a lot of idle choristers were allowed to set it on fire, by the reverent care of the custodians. At this time, near the beginning of the fifth-century work of Ravenna, the hoofs of Attila are treading down Europe, and he is driven back from Chalons to destroy Aquileia. He is Etzel in the Nibelungenlied. That date, 451, marks the first flight to the Lagunes, from Aquileia and other towns. Altinum was not finally destroyed till 641, by the Lombards. Then the episcopal seat was removed to the island of Torcello, and the inhabitants of the mainland city, giving up all hope of returning to their former homes, built their Duomo there. The Marchese Selvatico believes that that original church of the seventh century, partially, not entirely, restored in 1008, is now standing, "variously strengthened, refitted, and modified, but, on the whole, preserving its original aspect"—on the lonely islet to the north-east of Venice. Its architecture is Romanesque—round arches, but without cupolas over them, which are Byzantine: its mosaics are, or resemble Byzantine work, except that they are, as might be expected, ruder than those of Ravenna. At the east end is the Lord in Glory; He fills the apse of all Byzantine churches; at the west is the Last Judgment, already referred to. It is, as far as I can discover, after some inquiry, the earliest existing attempt at representing that inconceivable event. It is the earliest on record, unless we except the celebrated painting of Methodius, the Apostle of Thrace and the Danube, made for Bogoris, king of Bulgaria, about 850. Here the Penal Lake of Fire is represented as a red stream, or river of the wrath of God, flowing from under the Throne. There are no details of torment, and none of that fantastic play with terror which characterize Gothic work in after-days. But Torcello is the mother city of Venice. And as the Lombards of the seventh century drove the dwellers in Altinum to make their nests in the sea, in halcyon fashion, at Torcello and Rio Alto (Rialto, the earliest centre of Venice);—so they settled at Verona themselves. And, first of all barbarians (for the Ostrogoths seem to have employed Byzantines, and done but little themselves)—they set to work at bas-relief at once; and as hard as they could. In Art, as in all things, this great and still unconquered race, noblest of Southern Teutonry, worked hard and spared not; neither their brains and imagination, nor their hammer and chisel, nor their axe and sword, ever rested till the days of Pepin and Charlemagne. Mr. Kingsley has chosen Longobards or Lombards (Longbeards) as his ideal figures of Goths or Teutons, in Hypatia. I remember, he was supposed to have got into disgrace by that work. He gives a partly unfavourable view of the great Cyril of Alexandria; but the absolute perfection of that prelate's character is not part of our creed; and I really think the excellence of the book, in its pictures of Alexandria, its philosophies, and its great Christian work and institutions, make it fit reading for all. In short, it is the only readable picture we can get of the time and place; as Scott's Count Robert of Paris contains the only description in our language of the court of the Byzantine Empire. I used to have a list of historical novels for my Oxford pupils, to be taken along with their text-books, like Harvey sauce with cold mutton, and I should be glad to furnish anybody with it.* But for the Lombard carvers. These

---

* For Middle-Age Period—*Count Robert of Paris*; Scott's *Betrothed*, and *Talisman, Ivanhoe, Quentin Durward, Anne of Geierstein;* Bulwer's *Harold, Last of the Barons;* Kingsley's *Hypatia;* G. Eliot's *Romola.*

unknown workers are a school, or a set of men of the greatest importance in Art-history, and in all history. For they laid the foundation of all that drawing of form, all that sense of power to record, and teaching by representative record, which inspired Nicolo Pisano, and Giunto Pisano, and Cimabue, and Giotto, when Painting awoke soon after Sculpture. The order of the Arts is always the same. Architecture comes first in time, because you must have a roof to live under first; then Sculpture, because it is human nature to cut one's beams and stones about —at all events, it was Lombard nature; then Painting, when one has learnt enough of form from Sculpture to want to put on a little colour. The sleeping arts are like the sleeping Eumenides; they call each other up—ἔγειρ'· ἔγειρε καὶ σύ τήνδε· ἐγὼ δὲ σε. "Up, wake thou her, as I wake thee." So, undoubtedly, goes the history of sculpture and painting at Pavia, Verona, and Pisa; at Florence, and then at last in Venice.*

The early authority for the history of the Lombards is one of themselves. I believe I have done a thing not frequently done: I have read nearly all

---

* San Michele at Pavia is not of later date than the seventh century, about the date of the oldest part of Torcello; S. Zenone near four centuries later.

through Paul Warnefridus the Deacon, and live to tell the tale. Professor Kingsley has read the story of Ayo and Ibor, and the origin of the name Longbeard, in Book I.; and he tells it again beautifully in Wulf's Saga, in Hypatia. But it is possible he may not have extended his studies very far into a rather unpromising chronicle in rather curious Latin. I cannot find room now to say more about the Deacon, except that he seems to have been a knight or gentleman of the blood of Alboin, with whom his great-grandfather crossed the Alps; that he shared in the ruin of the Lombard rule in northern Italy by Pepin; that he retained, unbroken, his fealty to Didier or Desiderius, the last Lombard king; that he was carried away into Gaul as a prisoner, escaped to Italy again, became a Benedictine monk at Monte Casino, and there wrote his chronicle, with many copies of Latin verses, ingenious and pious. Altogether he must have been a true, intelligent and valiant sort of man; and one may partly see in his works the extraordinary comfort and blessing the convent afforded in those dreadful times, to any one who was in the position of anvil rather than of hammer. One or the other a man must be, at many periods of the world's history. The Lombard exile had no longer home or nation; but the brotherhood of Benedict was both to him : and his thankful duty to the founder of his order is commemorated in such hexameters and pentameters as never perhaps were conceived before or since by any of the sons of men.

Well, he says, his ancestors came from the isle of Gothland in the Baltic, called Scandia. They come within range of geography and chronology somewhere on the Danube in Noricum, not far from Vienna; and in the time of Odoacer (*i.e.*, about 476). He was slain by Theodoric about twenty years after. In April, 568, they accept the invitation of Narses (see Gibbon), and Alboin leads them across the Noric Alps, somewhere about Friuli or Forum Julii (not the other Forum Julii, Frejus on the other side of Italy). They are already good smiths and craftsmen in metal—one curious and grim relic of the handiwork of that day the Deacon says he has seen King Rachis show to a party of friends—the goblet or " scala " made from the gold-mounted skull of Cunimund, slain by Alboin, as Gibbon narrates. Great progress in Art and craft were made in Alboin's time, says the Deacon, and his name and glory were long dear to his people. His occasional acts of mercy and magnanimity are dwelt on, as Gibbon speaks only of his ferocity, &c. Pavia and Verona are the Lombard capitals: they seem to have been converted from

Arianism about the time of Gregory the Great; the baptism of Agilulf and Theodolinda was commemorated in a strange mosaic, of which a plate is given in *Ciampini's Vetera Monumenta.** It looks just as if they were being boiled. The early story of Theodolinda's wooing by her first husband, and her second choice of Agilulf, is as fresh and charming as any knightly tale I ever read. Now the thing to observe is that, at Verona, these hammer-men got among the marbles of the Alps, and saw examples of marble-carving. At it they went straightway. Smith turns sculptor; their skill in craft distinguishes them from former invaders of Italy: and it seems to me to mark their Scandinavian origin. They can learn and imitate and invent; they can make as well as break; above all they have the imaginative, creative, or poetic gift; and all the wildness of the northern fancy is theirs. The great Artist-race of the world have just won their land—the first things that interest them in it are the churches, and the story of the Christian faith in them. And these Verona photographs show the sort of work they did. Observe the door and base of the wheel window,—it is the type of a Romanesque church. And now try to forget the ugly colours and blank darkness of the photograph,

* *Tab.* iii. Part I. p. 20.

and think of all this as a dazzling mass of rose and white marble, like the Doge's Palace at Venice; strong like a fortress; coloured like a palace; a gallery of Art and a school of symbolism; a record of Christian history. For here historic and symbolic Art begin together in the service of God; and all the chief facts and events of the Faith were narrated in the bas-reliefs of this church, and on the castings of its bronze doors—probably the most ancient of all Christian works of the kind. The men who did these were the precursors, or in some sense the ancestors, of the great Florentine succession from Giotto to Michael Angelo. Their work is far different in spirit from Byzantine carving. With less sense of beauty, and less accurate perfection in masonry, it has far more life, novelty, variety of fancy, and energy of representation. There is an eastern quietude, and obedience to rules which alter not, in the Byzantine work; it is graceful and fixed, restrained by beautiful but unrelaxing conventionality: it is the work of an exhausted race of Christians. But the Lombard building and carving is the work of fighting and conquering Christians; it bears the stamp of the hunter and the soldier. In the work of S. Zenone, scriptural histories are mingled with knights in combat, and the weird

"Chase of Theodoric"—now utterly effaced by mere idle mischief. As with Clovis on the Rhine, so here with Astulf or Agilulf, the faith has prevailed with the conquering race and will share its power. "He that hath no sword, let him sell his garment and buy one." It is so here; the garment of Roman civilization is sold, and the Gothic war-sword is bought indeed.

And now we pass to Pisa. Nicolo Pisano's career centres about 1250. I pass by Sicilian Art, mainly because I do not know enough about it; but for other good reasons also. In the first place, no great school of drawing and painting is derived from it, it is a kind of *cul de sac*, and leads nowhere; though, as Lord Lothian observes, the same collision occurs in Sicily, between ancient Byzantine Art of the highest character, and the vigour of Northmen and Saracens, which occurred in Verona and Venice, between Byzantine work and Saracen or Lombard. The spirit of the North and the spirit of the East strive equally in both Venice and Sicily. Frederick II. ornamented Sicily with many buildings, decorated with statues, mosaics and frescoes by unknown artists anterior to Antelami, or Giunto of Pisa, or Guido of Siena; but they had no successors. And books of good information on the historical period of painting after Cimabue are so common, that I shall only give the barest skeleton of Art history;—a skeleton "far too naked to be shamed"—of mere names in order, with leading characteristics. The two best standard works of modern authority are Wornum's *Epochs of Painting* and Crowe and Cavalcaselle's *History of Italian Painting*.

The names of Buschetto (end of eleventh century) and Nicolo Pisano, whose career centres in 1250, should be remembered:* the one as the architect of the Cathedral of Pisa and its Baptistery and leaning Campanile; the other as the great sculptor who brought form and drawing within reach in Tuscany, retaining all the Lombard expression and energy, but drawing science, and correctness from study of ancient models. Giunto of Pisa and Guido of Siena are named the earliest painters of Italy. Torrita, or the monk Jacobus designed the mosaics of the Baptistery of Florence. Then, about 1270, Cimabue broke away finally from the old semi-Byzantine school of gold backgrounds and traditional treatment, and so caused the death of poor Margheritone, its last Italian professor. But he did a still greater service to Art in recognizing the powers of Giotto,

* Vasari says Nicolo studied under some Greek sculptors who were working in the Duomo of Pisa (Della Valle says he learnt from native Pisans). A great sarcophagus, with the Calydonian boar-hunt, and nude and draped figures, is mentioned.

and training him to his great work; he not only reigned but chose his successor.

If, as is asserted, the Middle Ages centre in Dante, they centre also in Giotto, his friend and companion, scarcely his inferior in power. It is now, I am happy to say, quite easy to get photographs from the works of Giotto and the early schools. He is the first of the universal artists, who were perhaps goldsmiths, architects, engineers, engravers, sculptors, and painters in all vehicles; who could design cathedrals and paint frescoes on their own walls, like Leonardo, or Durer, or Michael Angelo. Cimabue was nobly born and attained notice and influence early. His advance in all before him is marked. But the best thing he did was to discover, and value, and educate to surpass himself, the shepherd's boy, whom he found one day drawing a ram's head on a tile in the hill pastures that look down on Valdarno. Giotto's chief works are at Padua and Assisi—some remain at Rome; and at Ravenna one of the most beautiful contrasts in the world is in St. Giovanni Evangelista; where one of the chapels is ornamented like the Arena at Padua, with Giotto's blue backgrounds and lovely faces (I never was so struck as this year by their great beauty);—and the solemn mosaics of the roof are all in Tyrian purple and sea green. His greatest architectural monument is the Campanile at Florence; the Arena Chapel at Padua gives an idea of the universality of his powers. He was very ugly or irregular of feature, and seems to have enjoyed the circumstance greatly. He never left off making jokes, great and small. A century of Giotteschi, or disciples of his, succeeded him before any one again reached the mark he had made. Orgagna is the next to do so. As a colourist, to this day no man has excelled or can excel the qualities of the blonde faces one sees at Padua and Ravenna. His blues, warm whites, golden tints on hair and ornament, with many subtle uses of Indian red and other pigments, and various greens, all are matters of professional study to this day. There is a beautiful sketch by Lord Lindsay of the peaceful times in Padua, in the spring and summer of 1303, when Giotto, with wife and children, and Dante who knew in him one friend at least, rested "in breathless quiet after all their ills," hearing no more of the factions of Bianchi or Neri,—as the Arena frescoes went on extending all Summer through, over the walls of the little chapel in the fields, once the shambles of Roman holidays—to this day a Keblah and sacred place of pilgrimage for all who have followed, or who desire to follow, the steps of the first great Italian master.

LECTURE IV.

*FLORENTINE SUCCESSION OF PAINTERS
AND HISTORY OF SYMBOLISM AND
THE GROTESQUE.*

It is said to the disparagement of modern railways, that now-a-days there is no travelling at all, one only arrives, and is delivered like luggage. Contrariwise I hear it asserted, that in the old times one travelled a good deal, but frequently did not arrive, but was shot into the road like rubbish. I am not going into the rights of these counter-statements, but only want, by way of introduction, to indulge in a brief recollection of one of the arrivals of my life—the first sight of Pisa on an Italian evening. The day had been long, hot and exciting; there had been a row with an offensive Vetturino. I had transferred myself to the side of an old conductor on an old diligence, drawn by old horses, at five miles an hour, along a straight road, with a green canal by it, and a clumsily built, but gondola-looking boat, which made me think of Venice. It was dreamy and nice; but at last there came a turn in the road, and I saw the Baptistery and Duomo, and above them the leaning Campanile, all flaming, like rubies and red-hot gold against deep azure; with a vivid suddenness of impression, a purity and force of colour, and a rush of associations and history all at once, which I shall remember to the end of my days. It was not till afterwards that I recognized the grand situation of Pisa, between the mountains and the sea, or its slight analogy to Ravenna; I felt, as every one does feel at such times. I was in body then where I had been in spirit a hundred times, in presence of the second group of buildings in the world; if (which I doubt) St. Mark's is to be the first. We must pass this by. Remember, that the cathedral and other buildings were begun by Buschetto, at the end of the eleventh century; adorned by Nicolo Pisano up to the middle, or latter end of the thirteenth; that the Campo Santo, or burying-ground has on its walls the frescoes of Giotto, Orgagna, and Benozzo Gozzoli, especially the Triumph of Death, by Orgagna; and that within it rest the bones of Crusaders in the soil they won; the sacred soil of Jerusalem, which their fathers brought year by year in their galleys, therein to rest. Nicolo Pisano's career, I said, centres in 1250, and we pass from him to Cimabue and Giotto. There are so many and so good accounts of the progress of the earlier Florentine school; and the biographies of its members are, on the whole, so uneventful, that very brief sketches of them will suffice, up to the death of Ghirlandajo, and the beginning of his great pupil's career. These papers, originally delivered as lectures, cannot attempt anything like connected history, though they are an attempt to bring Art into closer contact with History. I have relied chiefly on the History of Florentine Art, by Messrs. Crowe and Cavalcaselle—a mine of information, and rich in original documents, and new facts. There can be no doubt that the Florentine school is the modern school of Drawing, as the Venetian is the world's school of Colour. And for any purposes of study below those of a matured and professional painter, the works and history of the student-masters, from Giotto to the early mind of Rafael, are excellent sources of knowledge, and the best education for awakened feeling. These men's works are their history: how they were worried by patrons and half-starved in monasteries—fed on stale leavings, like the Ghirlandajos, or entirely on cheese, like Paul Uccello; how Masaccio got into debt for common necessaries, and never paid, or was paid; and how monks and abbots habitually whitewashed frescoes over with the energy of churchwardens; all this is a lamentation and an ancient tale of wrong, which we cannot linger over: it is gossip, though it is sometimes sad, and often amusing. Let me name a succession of men, who seem to me, on the whole, the best to choose as typical or representative men, up to the youth of Rafael and Michael Angelo, and then we will go to our symbolism. Giotto* is the universal master, poet and craftsman, far in advance of all men of his time, *i.e.* from 1276 to 1336.

Orgagna,† or the three Arcagnuoli, or the Sienese Lorenzetti: whoever it was, and whatever number of men it was, who painted the frescoes in the Campo Santo at Pisa, represent Byzantine and Eastern asceticism and severity of religious thought. His, or their power of drawing, vigour of conception, and grasp of mind equal Giotto's; without his sense of pure beauty. The Loggia at Florence is Andrea Orgagna's design, and has no equal in the world.

---

* National Gallery, 276, 568 Wornum's Catalogue of 1867.
† National Gallery, 559, 570—578.

Date of Andrea's birth unknown—he was dead in 1376. Like Verrocchio, Leonardo, Ghirlandajo, and Dürer, he began as a goldsmith.

Fra Angelico,* Brother John of Fiesole, represents religious peace, devotion, hope, and happiness, without severity. He is the central Purist of the world, and the ideal and the spiritual meet in his works, simply because all his ideas were about blessed spirits— 1387 to 1455. His favourite pupil was Benozzo Gozzoli. His frescoes are still on the walls of the Convent of St. Mark, at Florence: almost as bright and fresh as when Savonarola studied them day by day, and Rafael, and Baccio della Porta, Fra Bartolomeo with him. He had no influence on naturalist Art, into which Benozzo Gozzoli quietly glided, but he is a representative man and painter in all senses of the word.

Masaccio is the evident precursor of Michael Angelo, though Ghirlandajo may be placed between them, having been for a time his actual master. Bodily action, like that of Greek statues, begins in earnest in Masaccio: he learnt much, probably, from Donatello: his great works of reference, studied by almost all masters from his time to ours, are in the Brancacci Chapel of the Carmine Church at

* National Gallery, 582, 663.

Florence. The Adam and Eve there, with the Baptism by St. Peter, are represented in Kugler, in Crowe and Cavalcaselle, and *passim*. The figure in the Baptism, called the Shivering Youth, is said by Count Lanzi, to form an era in Art. With it and the other works in the Carmine, Art strides definitely beyond Giotto. Had Masaccio lived longer, he would probably have anticipated the mountain naturalist landscape of Turner. Nothing is known of him, except that his name ended in 'accio—or, in other words, that everybody laughed at and bullied him all his life (1402?—1443). Paolo Uccello, Filippo Lippi, Lorenzo Ghiberti, and Masaccio, were all working at one time in Florence, close to each other; or, as to Filippo and Masaccio, at the same chapel, or even picture. I wonder if the old walls are haunted. Probably not; but anyhow, there is enough of the spirit of the painter left, in the faded frescoes which old Italy half destroyed by neglect, and young Italy thirsts to destroy by restoration.* Ghirlandajo's work is represented in the National Gallery only by No. 296—one of the most important pictures in the Gallery for the student. 1449 to 1498 embraces his life in Florence. For power of expression, of drawing the clothed form, of

---

* National Gallery, 626, his own portrait with red cap.

representing crowds of men in harmonious action, for variety of character, sense of beauty, rapidity of work, or careful tender elaboration—he is unsurpassed. He was Masaccio's best disciple; perhaps for a time, Michael Angelo's best master; but two such men never could live long in one studio, any more than Titian and Tintoret. The church of St. Trinita, with histories of St. Francis, and the frescoes of Sta Maria Novella (now, and I trust mercifully, repainted) contained in 1867, the best examples of Ghirlandajo's work in fresco yet remaining, unless it be the great Last Supper in S. Marco.

These men's works bring us to the study of the early drawings of Rafael and Michael Angelo. The photograph and autotype have brought these within almost everybody's reach; we shall see what use is made of the vast facilities for study, and the rapid and copious reproduction of artistic beauty, which are now afforded us. Careful, correct study in pen and ink, with hard pencil, and with brush and sepia from Rafael or Michael Angelesque autotypes, ought certainly to be added to our Art-school course. And those who will work at them for themselves, choosing the simplest things first, and contenting themselves with nothing short of *right* copy, or facsimile measured to the twentieth of an inch, will not fail of their reward. With the exception of Angelico, these earlier men are naturalists, delightedly painting or trying to paint all they see, rejoicing in their study and record of God's works. And in this spirit of observation, admiration and record, they are one with Turner and the modern school of landscape; who, finding their own modern life unlovely, could not write down its outward shows with the enjoyment of the Greek or the Italian; but betook themselves to the beauty of inanimate nature, and called on the spirit of the mountains. They got them away far off, and abode in the wilderness; they fled away, and for a time had some rest. The names I have given are only representative names, but many more might be given: Leonardo and Luini might be added, or even substituted for Michael Angelo and Rafael. But Tintoret and Veronese followed Michael Angelo; and the Venetian school, which I must not talk of now, has a tie to him in the high-reaching words of the former, Il disegno di Michel Angelo, é il colorito di Tiziano.—He is the central figure of Christian Art, as Dante in poetry: the most faithful to the greatest talents, from the beginning to the end.

SYMBOLISM AND THE GROTESQUE.

Now for our symbolism. The reason why I bring this subject regularly before you is that Art, as a matter of fact and historically speaking, is from its very beginning necessarily involved with it, and in two ways. First, because of the connexion of Art with letters, of representation with written language, of hieroglyphics with phonetics; and secondly, because, as a matter of fact, Art has been employed on symbolic teaching, principally religious, from the very earliest times of Art or of visible religious organization. "Symbol, σύμβολον, σύμβολα, tallies, the two halves of a coin or like object which any two contracting parties broke between them and preserved; hence a token or ticket; or a watchword, distinctive mark or formula; the creed of the Church, a sign by which one knows a thing," &c. That is the set of ideas which a reference to Liddell and Scott at once brings before us. This notion runs through them all; that the symbol is something put, for convenience, in the place of something of equal or greater value and importance, not now producible. Now words are signs or symbols, and stand for things like pictures. What is their relation to each other?

A sign or symbol, say logicians, is either *repre-*

sentative, indicates a thing to your mind, and makes you think of it—as a bunch of grapes over a house door, indicating wine, is called a publichouse sign; or it is *vicarious*, as a five-pound note stands for five sovereigns, and the five sovereigns stand for the labour of five men at a pound a week. Signs are also natural, as laughter and tears, or they are arbitrary. D-o-g might have meant cat if we had liked to make it so, only the ingenious little boy who said it spelt cat was in a minority of one. And talking of publichouse signs, they are arbitrary to a degree. Why should a pig and whistle, or a blue lion and bagpipes indicate the sale of liquor? One sees, of course, that grapes do; perhaps, the incongruity of the objects mentioned may artfully symbolize intoxication. This is one of those things evidently which no fellow, lecturer or other, can be expected to explain. But all hieroglyphic or picture-writing, is *representative* symbolism: while the spelt word composed of letters is a *vicarious* sign for the thing which it is a name of. The bunch of grapes reminds you of the juice of the vine, but you can't drink it; the piece of paper passes vicariously for the five pieces of gold, and you can spend it. So the picture teaches the spectators; the word passes current, for thought or thing.

Now word-making and picture-making go on together in the infancy of language: which implies poverty of words, and progress in supplying new words to express new thoughts. Savage orators are always figurative and symbolic; and people who live under civilization without using its advantages as they should, are always running into new forms of expression, which are generally called by the name of Slang. "Slang," says Mr. Ford in the *Handbook of Spain*, in describing the peculiar language of the Madrid bull-ring, "is nearly always metaphorical." I remember at the end of a Tennis-match, which had greatly interested all Oxford under-graduates in my time, hearing this remark, made by a friend of the winner—"Well, I suppose all the cards have landed their pots." That is to say, he supposed all the pack of men or cards who composed his circle, had landed, secured as it were by angling, their pots of money, as it were treasure-trove. I apprehend the extreme impropriety of the remark arose simply from the fact that the occasion was vulgar, and metaphor unnecessary; he had no new meaning to express, and he could have done without figure. But when Justice Ingleborough calls Die Vernon the heath-bell of Cheviot, he uses metaphor to convey a new idea in a right way previously unused. All of us, perhaps, know the value of simile in teaching. Those who are so employed must always keep numbers of trite comparisons and cut-and-dry illustrations by them as a sort of stock in trade. The more familiar idea is used to lead to, or take the place of the more recondite or important one; that is symbolism or the use of symbol. We need not go into the distinctions between words, as metaphor, parable, allegory—the result is the same in all.

Now, many Art-symbols are compounded arbitrarily, and like nothing in nature as wholes — (I have already said that their parts ought to be right resemblances of nature)—and being unlike anything in nature they are odd, and so the word grotesque comes to be applied to them. It is an Italian adjective, derived from κρύπτω,—crypt, place of concealment or cavern, says Prof. Mömmsen. Perhaps ideas of Pan and the Fauns, and such like cavern-haunting figures, combining noble and ignoble form, may be connected with it—at all events so many symbolic representations are grotesque in their appearance that the two terms naturally come together in my mind, and consequently in my lecture. And oddity and incongruity being especially dear to the Lombards, and all the higher Goths, the grotesque enters very largely into all northern Gothic. It is at Venice in particular, where Gothic and Byzantine meet, that the eastern temper may be seen to prevail, and the "grotesque laughter of the Goth" dies away from architecture. It is loud in Verona and Pavia; in Florence it is scarcely heard at all. To one coming from the south, it is at Ravenna that the first notes of the Gothic laughter are found, in S. Giovanni and the Duomo piers. We are right in connecting grotesque with Gothic, when it means play of humour, enjoyment of incongruity, and natural delight in putting the wrong thing in the wrong place, to see what it is like when there. Dr. Riccabocca's getting into the stocks on that principle is a touch of genuine northern Gothic. Dante's Demons, and also Shakspeare's Witches are great examples of serious Gothic grotesque; also Dominie Sampson, and the later passages in the life of David Deans, &c. In eye-Art the grotesque passes through Dürer, Holbein and the architectural carvers, away into the more serious caricature; through Hogarth and Cruikshank to some works of Leech, and many of Tenniel.

Now to go back to letter-symbols and picture-symbols. Some of the earliest historical records are representative bas-reliefs, in Egypt, and also I think in Assyria. In these Art does not illustrate history, it *is* the history; the record is all picture. In the historical tablets or records of conquest at Wady Maghara, in Sinai, Soris swings his cleaver in relief over heaps of prostrate enemies, making history in the usual way; and besides that there are representations of the animals and productions of the conquered countries. So Rameses at Aboo Simbel. This is writing by pictures, and we want to get from that to writing in letters, for this reason: that the letters represent sounds, and are interchangeable for any number of words. Any letter will fit; and the hieroglyphs represent things, and are not so conveniently interchangeable. The letters are not like anything in nature, and can be used, therefore, equally for the names of anything in nature; and the pictures or hieroglyphics are more like one thing than another. Now the progress into letters must have been something like that from the old stereotype block book to use of moveable types. In the block-book, you know, all the text in a page was like a picture, and you could not use the letters of one page to make up the words of another; you can do it with moveable types. Well, how were the hieroglyphic picture-blocks broken up into moveable letters? By making a certain number of them represent sounds and not things, and so forming an alphabet of sound-letters. And they were arranged to mean sounds and not things, thus: *the initial sound* of the name of a thing was held to be meant always by the hieroglyphic picture of that thing. Beth in Hebrew, Beit in Arabic, and for aught I know, Booth in English, all mean house, roof, shelter, &c. The initial sound of the name Beth is B. The old hieroglyphic picture of Beth, a house or shelter, ב is made to mean the B sound. (I may say that the letter is somewhat like the black camel or goats-hair screens which the Bedouin use for tents, taken in perspective; and that in common Arabic the tent is called 'the house'). א (Aleph) Ox is clearly a rude sketch of that quadruped seen in perspective, Gimel is the neck, head, and foreleg of the camel; Sin or Shin, the coils of the serpent, &c. However, picture-writing had made vast progress before the phonetic systems, and it is doubtless connected with the great Egyptian gift of powerful outline. Professor Rawlinson says it was not abandoned in Egypt till Christianity introduced the Coptic—an alphabetic writing between Greek and Egyptian.

But I want to point out the connexion of Christian symbolism: how the same subjects were repeated for teaching from age to age by different races. The first and great one, ordained by special revelation, sanctioned and commanded on Mount Sinai, is the Cherub. Two forms there certainly were of it : one known only to the priests, represented on the Ark, probably recognized by Ezekiel, as a priest, in his first Vision; another and popular form of it was wrought on the Temple doors, and veil, and known to the people generally. The whole subject is connected with Assyrian and Egyptian symbolism. But there is no doubt that it is continued in Veronese griffinism, for cherub is gryps, griffin ; and the wheel by the Veronese cherub, or griffin, is a reference to the Vision in the opening chapter of Ezekiel. But I must refer you to *Modern Painters*, Vol. III., and to Dr. Hayman's article in Smith's "Biblical Dictionary" on the subject. We have no time for modern use or misuse of angelic, or cherubic forms in Art; but the Lombard monsters are scriptural to all intents and purposes.

This is a list of the earlier Christian symbols found in the Catacombs :—First, those not directly scriptural. The Fish, as an anagram for our Lord's name : the Ship of Souls, or of the soul, unless it be considered as an Ark, and so a scriptural emblem—this is found repeatedly in ancient sepulchral work. The Cathedral of Torcello is itself a symbolic temple-ship; and the Navicella of Giotto at Rome is the great example of this emblem. With these, the anchor and lyre, the eagle and chariot rarely; the phœnix, pelican, and peacock. The hand is found at Ravenna, and in sarcophagi, as representing the First Person of the Trinity. Chief scriptural symbols are the Good Shepherd, earliest of all; the fish, as typical of the Christian soul; the vine, lamb, dove, and olive; the cock, and palm-branch: also the lion, dragon, and serpent. Of symbolic or parabolic events, the Agape of bread and fish, or the fish bearing loaves; Moses and the Rock; the Holy Children; Noah in his square chest, or ark; Daniel with the lions; Jonah, with gourd or whale; Elijah in his chariot; Pharaoh and the Red Sea, are of the earliest date of Christian Art. Sometimes they are beautifully done, sometimes grotesquely, but always they do mean this; that the sound sleepers beneath the tufa arches slept in Christ; holding by Him, as foretold in the Law, and by the Prophets. Since 410, says Dr. Mömmsen, no corpse has been deposited in the Catacombs; if it be so, all who lie there are united in one faith and hope. And the burden of all Christian symbolism is first Christ, both God and Man, as foreshadowed in the Law; and foretold by the Prophets; then Christ crucified,

God submitting to death and conquering death for man, and therein all pain or foretaste of death.

These typical subjects, then, are referred to in all Christian Art work in Catacombs, Ravenna, Verona, and so on down to Ammergau. But the great Christian symbol comes next for us; and we cannot pass it, for it faces us as soon as the Catacombs are closed, in the early work of Ravenna. I may say, that no Cross with the least pretence to antiquity occurs in the Catacombs at all, on the highly trustworthy testimony of Father Martigny (whose "Dictionary of Christian Antiquities" appears to be the best and readiest of all manuals of sacred archæology.) It may be that the Cross was used in private before Constantine; it probably could not be used in public before he abolished the shameful punishment of crucifixion. Like Christian adoption of Pagan flower ornament, &c., for tombs, this was part of the caution of times of persecution. From his time it was used as a symbol of our Lord's Humanity, with or without reference to His Death as a part of His Humanity. The earliest Crosses, as that called the Lateran (which, I believe, to be similar to those first erected or inlaid by Constantine, in his Baptistery, or elsewhere) are Baptismal Crosses; the Four Rivers of Baptism are represented flowing from the Cross-foot, and derived from the Holy Dove, which is always placed above the Cross. By one side of the healing waters are the Lambs of the Christian congregation: while the stag, representing the outer Gentile desiring Baptism into the Faith, stands on the other. The Cross is in its first use the symbol of Baptism into the Lord's death, or death with Him. The early use at Ravenna is remarkable: for there and up to the sixth century it stands truly as a symbol representing the Person of the Lord, rather than the manner of His Death. I think this falls in with the view which late inquiries have led me to as to the earliest origin of the Christian use of the Cross as a symbol. The first use of it derives, I think, from the monogram of the Lord's name; and represents His Person, as at Ravenna; standing for His Humanity, for the sacrifice, or humiliation, of His Life and Death taken as one. Most of us know that the ☧ or St. Andrew's Cross is exchanged into the upright ☧ in the majority of inscriptions, about the end of the third century. That marks the transition from the letter-monogram of the Lord's name, to the symbol which represented alike His Person, His Life, and His Death, as the mind desired to contemplate them. There is a mosaic in St. Apollinaris in Classe at Ravenna, of great doctrinal importance. It represents the Transfiguration; and in it the Hand is above all, as the First Person; the Cross, ornamented and jewelled, as it were, to the utmost power of the mosaicist, stands for the Second; and this personification is repeated till the seventh century. But, meanwhile, from the fifth, attention was more strongly fixed on the manner of the Lord's Death; and in the sixth century the Lamb is added to the Cross, and placed on the altar. Sometimes he is represented as wounded, as in the Apocalyptic vision. The earliest representation of the Crucifixion, setting aside the hideous Graffito of the Palatine, is that in the ancient Syriac MS. of the Laurentian Library at Florence—a work unique and matchless, with twenty-four wonderful miniatures (I think)—and distinguished from all others by this detail,—that the soldiers in its picture of the Crucifixion are not drawing lots, or casting dice for the coat without seam, but playing at mora for it on their fingers. This is probably the very first instance of a representation of the Crucifixion; and like many early ones, it is joined to a picture of the Resurrection. Of course, there is the widest practical difference between it and what is called the use of the separate crucifix as an object of devotion in later days. Till the seventh century, the nearest approach to the single crucifix in public use, was the crowned Lamb bearing a Cross, placed at the intersection of the limbs of the rood, or station-cross, as in the Crosses of the Vatican and of Velitræ. Then at the Quinisext Council, or Council in' Trullo, (in a round domed chamber at Constantinople) at the end of the seventh century—it is finally ordered that the human figure of our Lord be placed henceforth on church crosses "instead of the Lamb of former times." In the Cross of Mayence, I think, the Lamb is on one side of the Tree, the crucified form on the other; in the Cross of Velitræ the Lamb has the symbols of the Four Evangelists on the reverse. These come into their most frequent use about the sixth century.*

These lectures, however, are concerned rather with art than archæology; and I have touched on this subject because representations of our Lord's death form a part of the illuminations or miniatures of almost all sacred MSS. from the seventh or eighth century; and partly to draw a distinction which already exists, I suppose, in most of our minds. The object of these representations may be the

* This whole subject is admirably worked out in some papers in DIDRON'S *Annales Archéologiques*, vols. xxvi, xxvii., by M. Grimoald de St. Laurent.

sincere and solemn commemoration of the central event of the World's history; and the equally solemn assertion of the mystery of our Lord's humanity and death. Or it may be that of exciting passionate emotion by representing His bodily sufferings and physical pain. With the former object, I apprehend, it is admissible and permissible, and consistent with the feeling of our Church: with the latter I do not think it is so. Something, at least, should be conceded to the feeling of Puritan Christianity; and it should not be forgotten that only two, possibly three crucifixes, are now known to exist among the eighty millions of the Greek Church; and those secluded in monasteries as sacred relics, rather than applied to any use of worship.* Of course, as soon as it was enjoined by the church as a subject of painting, it became the most frequent of all; in MSS., in fresco, and mosaics, in enamels, and carvings; at last, it was set forth in mysteries, or acted pictures, from Holy Scripture. It is adopted at Verona by the Lombard sculptors, who follow the old custom of representing the Lord on the Cross, robed and crowned as King and Priest (as in the ancient crucifix, called the Face of Lucca.) They place the Lamb, however, on the keystone, over the door of

* See the Rev. T. TOZER's *Travels in Albania and Greece.*

the Duomo; and on the front and bronze gates of S. Zenone they repeat the ancient symbolisms; type and antitype, as in the Catacombs. Adam and Eve are set to plough and distaff; Noah stands in his square "arca," as of old; and the Angel stays the hand of Abraham, armed with a formidable straight Gothic sword: the Brazen Serpent is also crucified on the gates.

Noah—Callixtine Catacomb.

The Lombard Noah—
Doors of S. Zenone.

From the Lombard work the transition to the MSS. &c., is easy; and in both, plain history-pictures of events in the text accompany, and often prevail over symbolism; and mere fanciful ornament or pleasure in beautiful curves and colours often prevails in turn. We have not room to talk of MSS.

now. I had rather go on straight to the plays or exhibitions which, as it seems to me, stood in the place of paintings and illuminated MSS. for the instruction of the poor. From their earliest date their most prominent subject of representation was the mystery of the Lord's death. It seems that we only know, or have heard scattered and dubious accounts of the dark side of those representations, and that they were rightly permitted as a means of popular instruction, much needed before the invention of printing. A knight or nobleman might not read MS. very fluently (and observe, any one who has ever tried to read an old MS. will know that the varying contractions and abbreviations used in every line must have made fluent reading rather rare and difficult); consequently, if the knight could afford it, he had his illuminated Evangeliary or Psalter or Missal, in which he found explanatory pictures with the text, of principal events, with every possible device of colour and fanciful design for pleasure in his reading. The poor man had not this advantage; and therefore, besides the church frescoes or mosaics, these acted pictures were allowed him; which, with proper explanations from his priest, or a regular chorus during the performance, would really give him a certain acquaintance with the main facts of the Old and New Testament, and especially with the connection, by type and prophecy, between the Old Testament and the New. The mystery-plays were by no means mere licensed outbursts of blasphemy. They have been represented as a kind of safety-valve for disbelief and discontent; a permitted Saturnalia of mockery and licence. This generally permits the writer or speaker a good deal of abuse of the Roman Catholic Church, which the subject, in fact, does not call for, and which is highly unnecessary. This was forcibly brought home to me during a visit to Ober-Ammergau and the Passion-play last year, 9th July. I had expected an appeal to emotion, like that of the Seven Stations at Nuremberg — a representation, not probably offensive, but painful, and to be borne with and allowed for. What I found was a course of instruction by acted pictures, in the typical nature of persons and events in the Old Testament. The first object and tendency of the whole thing seemed doctrinal teaching; and that of a character which I must style plain Bible teaching; such as formed a great part of the Oxford pass-examination in Divinity, when that was. The Law and the Prophets and the history of Israel and its characters were set forth to the people as foreshowing the Gospel. Each scene of the Passion was preceded in the Passions-Vorstellung by its typical scene from Hebrew history, expounded always to the people in recitation or choric hymn, with noble voices and modest gesture. The argument of the whole was the Humanity and Death of God for Man's sake, to atone for sin and make an end of evil; and the witness of history thereto. It began with the Fall of Man and the Vision of the Cross of Sacrifice, it ended with the Lord's Ascension. And the whole representation is a relic of the Church's symbolic or pictorial teaching from the beginning.

Once more; the ancient themes of sepulchral or church decoration are the Law, History, and Prophecies of the Hebrew Race, as pointing to the Gospel; and the Lord's appearance and Miracles of Mercy as representing the Gospel. His Death is understood for the four first centuries, then symbolized, then openly represented. The first painted lessons of Christian Hope are in the Catacombs, where the Lord's own similitudes of himself are repeated in the form of the Good Shepherd and the Vine. Then about the end of the fourth century, a man of considerable genius, or at least of spirit both devout and artistic, St. Paulinus of Nola, took up the idea of pictorial teaching in earnest. Many churches and Christian sepulchres were painted, probably repainted, in his time. He had no sort of notion of image-worship, or of stimulating devotion by appeal to beauty, or by representation of bodily pain, or anything of the kind. His motto or leading idea, expressed in one of his odd hexameters was *Lex antiqua Novam firmat, veterem Nova complet* (or "The old Dispensation bears witness to the Gospel which fulfils it"), and that is the principle, the traditional theme of Christian symbolism from the Catacombs to Ammergau. Melchisedek's sacrifice, and that of Abel are added to the list at Ravenna, in a most important mosaic in St. Vitale. St. Paulinus' catalogue of emblems contributes also the History of Joseph and the Passage of the Red Sea, and in early mosaics at Ravenna, and in the first MSS. the Jordan as the River of Baptism unto death in Christ takes its part. The anagrammatic fish, the dove in all its meanings, the palm and peacock, the fish and bread, the lamb in both its senses, the four rivers, &c., are all emblems of all Christian ages: and of these the Old Testament types, Isaac, Joseph, Jonah, Daniel, the Bread, the Rock, Elijah, &c., are duly repeated at Ammergau. That is what the Passion-play really is; the ancient Bible-teaching of the middle ages; and those who were so taught, and paid earnest attention, were taught very well.

The old traditional symbolism seems to be thought of no more: though great works like Hunt's Scapegoat, or Ary Scheffer's Christus Consolator, in some degree take its place. It may revive with modifications, for the feeling in favour of church decoration by fresco and mosaic is renewing itself, I trust, rather vigorously. A good deal is doing in Yorkshire. I may speak of some works by a painter, well-known to painters, and best valued by his brethren, Mr. Spencer Stanhope. I went to see his works in a little grey church on a windy hill, not long built, but weather-worn already, looking to the moors above the Vale of Barnsley. Hoyland Swaine Church, they call it. There was some of the best conventional flower-ornament I ever saw, and a grand fresco in the chancel, Our Lord adored by Angels, filling the walls and roof. There is no doubt that if church decoration goes on in fresco and mosaic, the painters and sculptors must and will go back to the ancient Græco-Roman work of the Catacombs and Christian Sarcophagi, for the original subjects which appeal from the Gospel to the Law.

So much for the past of Christian symbolism, I trust it has a future before it also. And now for the kindred subject of which all Gothic work is so full. The Grotesque, as we said, implied sport of mind ; this

English people generally call humour, and connect it with laughter. But in Italy, and to a great extent in Germany, it is not necessarily ludicrous. Rafaelesque or cinque-cento grotesques are graceful and fanciful, by no means laughable or even ironical; nor yet is much Venetian work of this nature, nor are Holbein's religious woodcuts. The grotesque either arises from the contrast between Art and the Actual, in northern climates, where they are painfully opposed; or, from the play of a great workman's mind, as when he uses his full powers for the time only to record some wandering of his fancy, as Durer so frequently does. He is the great master of the serious grotesque. Dr. Woltman says he is dearer to Germany for his faults, the extraordinary flights of fancy, which are so peculiarly German. I can only mention two of his works here, both which are fairly intelligible, and are probably well-known to most of us—the Knight and Death, which appears to me to represent the mournful ending of human power and valour, whether it be meant to suggest hope in death, or deserved destruction; and the Melancholy which stands for the brooding toil of human thought and labour.

Holbein comes about twenty-five years after Durer, and I shall speak hereafter of his grotesques of the Dance of Death, the Indulgence-mongers, and Christ the True Light. The effect of the two latter on the mind of Germany at the Reformation is said to have been very great. One is the most vigorous assertion of the personal illumination or direction of the human spirit into necessary truth, in answer to prayer and by the grace of "Christ the true Light" —the other as mightily proclaims the efficiency of personal repentance, like that of Manasses or David; since indulgences and pardons are sold like merchandise, and the poor cannot buy them: the gist of the picture is not so much the buying or selling of God's forgiveness, as the vain cry of the helpless beggar to the indulgence-dealer to take away his sins without money down. This woodcut opens the old curious question of the comparative force of impression in poetry or painting. There is a contemporaneous flash of various converging ideas through the eye into the brain at the instant, which is conveyed by such works as these, and which seems to have a subtle and piercing force even beyond poetry.

The Dance of Death is associated with Holbein's wall-painting at Basle; of course, it is not the only one; that at Lucerne will be remembered, and it was a common subject in the middle ages. People walked with contented interest under the permanent public sermon on their own death, as a thing they did not greatly fear. But this carries us once more back to Pisa and Orgagna, and the tremendous Triumph of Death, the Judgment and Inferno of that man intolerably severe. There are photographs of this last now to be had without difficulty. You will see by it that the Florentine was less merciful of conception than the German, who had not been sharpened by civic feud and strife of cities, house against house. The pitch of Italian hatred in the middle ages has probably not been reached since; let us hope not. And here, too, you see a beginning of the tendency to seek a second Mediator in the Blessed Virgin, and implore her to save men from Her Son— as He also may have been by trembling minds to save them from His Father. The composition of Orgagna's Judgment is compared by Messrs. Crowe and Cavalcaselle to that of the Sistine. Both in an important sense of the word are grotesques; for the word really applies to representations where the power of the workman necessarily falls short of an unattainable and inexpressible subject.

One work there is of Michael Angelo's, which may do well as a crowning example of the serious grotesque, like Durer's Knight; and it also deals with the most important of all subjects, and gives us the great master's strange and mystic view of the Act of Death. I know that it is attributed by Kügler to the obscure Rosso Fiorentino, but I really think, it is only because the same transparent brown has been used in it, which is employed in a picture of Rosso's in the Uffizi. No man but Michael Angelo could have painted the original of those faces; and what is more, the cartoon of the Bathing Soldiers has some hard features in it, which are, I am sure, by the same hand as the Fates.

This is what I wrote of it, long ago, from the picture:—Three mighty spinning women; aged beyond the ages; wrinkled but not withered; stronger than men or the children of men; awful rather than terrible. One stands a little behind: it is she who metes out the length of the thread of life; and her task is over, the appointed span is all past. Her mouth is open, calling the name by which immortals know the soul whose hour is come. There is a trace of suspense and pain in her expression. She who spins has turned her face from the thread, her work too being done; and her eyes meet those of the fury with the abhorred shears. The latter is no fiend or hateful Erinnys in the mind of Buonarotti; both the sisters have a far-away look of strange pity; so distant and so faint, it reminds one no more of human tenderness than the evening Alpenglüth recalls the sun's warmth. Yet it is there; and with it the lips are just moved in the dawn of a strange smile, as if to say: They who mourn unknowing shall yet understand. And the thread is between the shears, and the sinews of the strong fleshless hand are set, and it is closing them slowly; and still the grave eyes seek the sister's face, expressionless, impenetrable, irrefragable. "I am all that has been, and is, and shall be: and no man hath ever lifted up my veil," said the statue of Isis. It is as if Michael Angelo had indeed raised it, and looked steadily on what it covered.

LECTURE V.

RAFAEL AND MICHAEL ANGELO.

THE Laureate says that Arthur Hallam lies buried in Florence, "by unfamiliar Arno, and the dome of Brunelleschi"—the dome which Michael Angelo said he would not imitate, and could not surpass. I do not know how far, or in what sense, Florence is unfamiliar to many English people. There are many unforgotten dead who lie by unfamiliar Arno, and the river and the dome have pretty close and deep associations in many English minds. But Italy and her great cities are, mentally speaking, the property of Europe. Those of us who are taught to indulge in the dubious luxury of Thought or Imagination, have their portion by Arno and by Tiber. In England, as in France, Germany, and wherever men have thought, or hope, or brightness, or the spirit of the singer in them, they look to Italy, and we English, above all, to Venice, which belongs to us by right of Shakspeare and Byron, and all the outpouring of island verse, good, bad, and indifferent, which has gone forth over the Lagune. It would be curious to trace the mingled feeling of admiration and dislike, but still of mutual attraction, which has existed between Italy and England for the last five hundred years: for good or evil. I hope it has not been so much for evil as is implied in the well-known cinquecento proverb, "Inglese Italianato è un diavolo incarnato." Those who want to read a common-sense exposition of the difference of the two characters may consult Lord Macaulay's Essay on Machiavelli. And when you hear of a plain, common-sense account of a thing, you know it means about two-thirds of the truth, put with force, clearness, and a total disregard of the other third.

There are few terms, I think, which are more useful, or harder worked, or more generally bewildering, than the term Renaissance, or revival, or Renascence, as Professor Arnold prefers to call it. It has that inestimable quality of a new word, that everybody can use it as he likes—just like a new toy. Nobody knows exactly what it may or may not be applied to. Is it or was it a Renascence of Arts, or of letters, or of thought, or of inductive science, or of all of them? Then in what sense was the Art

Renascence of the fifteenth and sixteenth centuries a fresh birth or return to life? In Art especially, had nothing been done since Alaric and his Goths rushed in at the Salarian gate, and brought night down on Rome for three hundred years? That was the death-day of Græco-Roman Art, I have always said. But the previous lectures have all gone on the understanding that there was, in the course of the next thousand years, a succession of revivals of Art in various forms, some of them of extreme importance and beauty. First at Ravenna, then at Verona and Pavia, then in the earliest work of Venice and its mother city, Torcello—(the daughter is like Horace's young lady, *filia pulchrior*, and takes precedence of her mother in history) — then in Sicily and Pisa, and then at Florence, finally in Venetian oil-painting. I do not mention Rome, and have never talked of a Roman school: first because the true pictorial succession, of strong men in the right path inheriting each others' teaching, goes through Florence and Venice from Cimabue to Veronese: secondly, because all great artists formed in the north, were sure to go and work at Rome some part of their lives, and Rome was naturally rather the exhibition-room than the school of Italy. My use of the word Renaissance, in fact, is very like that indicated by Mr. Bryce in his admirable essay; (which let all students of history take with their *Hallam* or *Sismondi*). He dates the revival of learning and letters 1100-1400, and says that "though the fifteenth and sixteenth centuries are well chosen as the period when the transcendent influence of Greece began to work upon the world, there had long been in progress a great revival, not only of learning," but, as he subtly says, "of zeal for learning," which, being directed to Rome, he calls the Roman Renaissance. "It began," he says, in the twelfth century with the passionate study of the Institutes of Justinian—the thirteenth witnessed the rise of the "scholastic philosophy," and he rightly puts in the fourteenth the great masters of painting and of song, clustering round the sad strength of Dante. Two of our earlier lectures went to trace the Gothic revivals of painting, taught, or rather inspired, and called into glad and emulous action, by Byzantinism and the conventual relics of Græco-Roman skill; and we contended all through them that the forces of the Teutonic mind, owing much, did not owe all, to classical models. The absolutely new direction which the Christian faith gave to the forces of poetic thought was marked, we said from Professor Ruskin, by the vastly greater attention paid by Gothic-

Christian artists to the expression of the face.* The body in its health, and contented perfection to the Greek: the expression of the spirit, its longings and its passion, imperfection penetrated by inspiration, sorrow burning into beauty—that to the Florentine. To say that the latter owed much to the former, is only to say that he *was* the latter in time; and that he was not a fool. To say that the Florentine owed the Greek his greatest success and full perfectness, is altogether wrong. And that seems to me to be the great error of the end of the last century and the beginning of this one: to talk about the Middle Ages as if they were obscured by absolute and prevailing mental darkness, as well as by the darkness of physical suffering. This error has provoked, as you know, a very strong Gothic reaction in Art, which is still in full vigour, though its direction is changed: as we see by the poetry of Tennyson and Morris. I decline characterizing either of them in conventional praise; but Rossetti's painting and poetry, the lovely verse of his sister, Burne Jones and his strong and advancing school, Stanhope, Crane, Bateman, Clifford and the rest—these bear witness enough to the surviving forces of northern Art: I write down their names as they occur to me, without waiting to think

* See Frontispiece of Sibyl.

of more. And this we must all feel, and our own Gothic Renaissance enables us to give voice to it; that the strength of our art is English strength; that you can't turn an oak or a yew tree into an olive, although we may try to learn, or must rediscover for ourselves, some of the secrets of Greek greatness. I have a notion that greatness is greatness; and that it depends on eternal principles; and accordingly that it is not accurate to say we discover the secret of so-and-so's greatness, as if he had dropped half-a-crown in the street, and we had picked it up. The thing for us is to work our way, if possible, to the conditions under which greatness was found, and look to Him who makes great and small. But, anyhow, Goths, Saxons and Northmen we are, and we cannot be Athenians; and the true way to follow Athenians is not to go on for ever copying them, but work as they worked, from the nature which they saw. And if, as a people engaged in manufactures, we cannot see nature now, as Christian and Hopeful could not see Heaven under the shadow of Death "by reason of the impediment which attends this place"—and other places on the coal-field—then our first work is to make the sight of natural beauty more and more accessible to ourselves, the people, and bring it into our own reach in furniture and decoration of good design;

and preach to those beneath us, in faithful landscape, the painters' gospel of green fields. It is not much, but it is possible.

Now, we have before us to-day the two men whose names are most entirely associated in art with the Renaissance of the Cinque-Cento, the Greek Renaissance, or revival of Greek language and literature in particular. Greek Art had begun to be revived when Nicolo Pisano began its study; for Greek Art practically means, the closest study of the noblest natural forms, of men and women. The religious Reformation was a corollary or consequence of this Greek Revival, in Germany and England; being only a part, as the revival of letters was only a part, of that great expansion and outburst of the power and flower of the mind of man which took place in those two centuries. The religious side of the Renaissance may be said to be the German or Cis-Alpine side of it: and we will talk more of it, in entering on the subject of Dürer's and Holbein's great works. But in Italy, the new life of the human spirit became artistic and literary, not religious, for the life of its religion was trampled out. The Protestantism of Michael Angelo, inherited from Dante, nourished by Savonarola, shared by Contarini and the Venetians, might have changed the world, with Holbein's and Durer's, if Jesuitism, statecraft, and the Curia had not prevailed at Trent. The lesson Italy has left us from then to now, is that (Bryce, p. 330), "Exclusive devotion to Art and literature (when religion and politics are alike closed) cannot compensate for the departure of freedom and a national spirit, and the activity of civic life. A century after the golden days of Ariosto and Rafael, Italian literature had become frigid and affected, while Italian Art was dying of mannerism," and he might have added, in great part of Rafaelism. And though this inevitable Preface is too long already, I must just dismiss, with hearty dislike and contempt, the notion that tyranny or despotism nourish Art. Art must have some patron it is true; but its best patron is an educated people, taught to draw, or at least to know by eye, form as connected with function. You may have an age of Ptolemy with a despot; you have had an age of Phidias under a free people, that is to say, a people restrained by law at home, and necessity of combat abroad. With the death of liberty in Florence, Art died there; Michael Angelo would live there no longer, and no man rose after him. People seem to forget that all the conditions which made him were those of rather turbulent free cities.

It is easy to see what has made Rafael in all times a central figure among painters, and the central figure of popular art. He is the most artistic of artists: he was good and bright and beautiful himself: his soul had an entire delight in beauty, and there is hardly any sensual feeling in his work; such loveliness has seldom been set forth without impurity, even where there is passion in it—he is not answerable for all his followers. All life went easily and delightfully with him, himself a delight to all men and women, and he did not take life too easily, or give himself to delight. The earliest portraits, if they do not show the man perfectly, show why the man was loved, and why he was great. They are so gentle and deep-eyed, as of a man who has his share of power and command through love; who will also see and know and learn continually; who will not strive hard against the stream, but will mix with the water and make it sweeter. He was not mighty with the mightiest. Buonarotti, Titian, Tintoret, Velasquez, the spiritual impact of these men was not his; he had not the flame and heart, the passion, or insight of the sons of " fire and morning." But of all men he took learning most kindly, and would learn from all men and things. His endless industry is better understood perhaps than other men's, from the wide dispersion of his slighter works, as well as his finished pictures. We shall see directly, in going through what are rightly called the periods of his short life, the extraordinary bee-like facility of getting more knowledge from every man, and assimilating power always, and making other men's power his own; so that the Peruginesque early pictures are Rafael's own, and nowise Perugino's, and even the grim eye of Michael Angelo could hardly trace where, or how, the youth half-envied half-regarded had gently plagiarized, or let us say adopted, his thought. Here I should much like an excursus about plagiarism and its limits. Briefly, I should say that when you use another man's help openly and confessedly, to do some good thing which he has not done, and in fair probability would not do, you are free before the world of art and letters. But I am talking about Rafael, who learnt his art from all men, being strong enough to teach all.

These are the periods of his life, collated as neatly as I can manage it with that of Michael Angelo. For though these men were unconnected with each other in their personal history, and were scarcely even friends, they are the foremost men of their day, and are so near each other in time and place, and are so vividly contrasted with each other in powers and character and career, that they must always be taken together in Italian art-history. And one of the educational needs of our time is the careful and picturesque connection of art with history; that is to say, the connection of what the painter did with what he saw, and with the people he had round him. One book there is beyond others, which suits our period and subject almost exactly, though neither Michael Angelo nor Rafael appear in it. It is the novel of *Romola*, before-mentioned. I believe somebody said it was a very good book, very hard to read; a statement apparently wrung from the poor gentleman who wrote it by the necessities of reviewing. He must be a weak brother or sister who cannot read *Romola* from beginning to end, and that reader must be an inattentive one who cannot get from it such a picture of Florence and Florentines in Michael Angelo's youth, as shall strengthen him greatly in understanding Italian history.

In 1492 Columbus is waiting for ships for his first voyage; Lorenzo de' Medici is dying at Careggi near Florence; Michael Angelo Buonarotti, a boy of seventeen, has been studying for the last three years under his patronage, and has done a capital head of an old Faun, and a bas-relief of Centaurs.[*] He has been working in the Medici Gardens, the collection or

---

[*] One is now in the Uffizi at Florence, the other in the Casa Buonarotti.

museum in Oltrarno near the Pitti ; and he has studied Masaccio in the Carmine. In one or other of these places he has had his own personal good looks seriously impaired for life by the fist or mallet of the huge and envious bully Torrigiano, who has flattened his nose almost hopelessly. Perhaps he will think of it in after days, when Raphael's fair eyes and delicate face are stealing love and fame from him. Torrigiano will carve and model, fight manfully sometimes, rave and bully always, do or narrate about himself great deeds "among the island bears" in England ; whither he will go to work for Henry VII. and VIII., and where he may probably meet a Tedesco called Hans Holbein. Finally he will die as the fool dies ; break his statue of the Virgin in a fit of passion, not unreasonable ; be "examined," as Vasari mildly says, by the Inquisition of Seville, and starve himself to death in its dungeons. For Michael Angelo, men think he has no master ; he has been Domenico Ghirlandajo's pupil a year, but they did not get on ; or rather, the lad got on too fast, and drew with a strong line like Masaccio, and corrected his master's drawing so that you could not say he was far wrong ; and one studio would not hold them both. There is a very pretty boy playing about at Urbino, born nine years ago to John Santi,

or Sanzio, a good painter much regarded by the
Duke. They call him Rafael, and they say he will
make a draughtsman, and in two or three years more
he will go and begin to be immortal under Pietro
Perugino—they won't quarrel, one may be sure. But
in three dozen years and one the old master's eyes
will be strained once more, dim enough with tears
and time, at three score years and twelve, to finish
some of the work his dead pupil will have left behind.*
There is just ten years of time between the two young
masters—one is the square man, the other the round
one. All the great and true of all ages will respect
the corners of the elder; all men in all ages who
have capacity or understanding of tenderness or
loveliness will delight in the smoothness of the younger.
One is born into the evil time at endangered
Florence, and will take his share in what is going, if
need be; the other is safe among the hills, and will
early and late have the painter's immunity in war and
faction, like Giotto in earlier days. One is sharp-
tongued already, with his high-bred pithy speech,
though rather too silent on the whole: Ghirlandajo
could not bear his father's contempt for painting. He
is passionate and self-restrained; the other has no
very violent impulses, and life runs pleasantly in his

* Fresco in S. Severo, Perugia. *See* Robinson, p. 143.

veins; his art secures him awhile from evil passions. Just before Rafael goes to school with Perugino, Buonarotti will have to ride hard out of Florence, with, or some days before, the expelled Piero de' Medici; and will escape to Bologna or Venice. Ludovico Sforza (patron of Lionardo di Vinci, who knows not yet what a rival is at hand),—Sforza, Duke of Milan, and traitorous curse of Italy, is just going to invite the first French invasion, to which Piero will lend himself shamefully, by giving up Florentine fortresses; and to which Savonarola is pointing in his sermons, at St. Marco, as a tempest of deliverance. The great Dominican is at Careggi with Lorenzo; some say he has bid him "Loose Florence,* or God will not loose thy soul,"—and that Lorenzo defied him; a very dubious tale altogether. But this is the point which Hallam chooses "before," as he says, "the French lances are shining in the defiles of the Alps,"—to close the middle ages of Italian history. At this time, then, Alexander VI., the Borgia, the father of Cæsar and Lucrezia of blessed memory, is sitting in Rome, after much bribery, as Vicar of Christ on earth; and he is and represents in Rome, as surely as the Roman eagles did in Jerusalem, the Abomination of Desolation sitting in the Holy Place,

* Casa Guidi Windows.

where it ought not. Against him Savonarola has come from Ferrara to Florence to testify; Michael Angelo has heard him, and will not forget him, or ever fear Popes overmuch. But the exile with Piero, and also the escape to Bologna from Piero, must have freed him from the shame and horror of the sight in the great Piazza of Florence; when the Florentine prophet came forth racked near to death, to be hanged and burnt for denying the Deity of the father of Cæsar Borgia. The times were of the nature considered by M. Taine the most favourable for the production of great art. Everybody wore the finest clothes conceivable, and indulged in the grossest and most violent vices imaginable. He does not say that Angelo or Rafael did either; but then of course, they had the advantage of seeing other people do it. You will see, however, that Rafael's birth under ancestral government, and in a court; his isolation from the political life of a free city, or one which desired freedom; and his peaceful separated artistic-conventual life, going happily off with Pinturrichio to Siena to paint the great library—were all very different from Angelo's, who was bound to Piero de' Medici for his father's sake; to Savonarola by faith and conviction; and to Florence, which exiled the one man, and hanged the other, by civic patriotism and love of home. The noble of once-free Florence could not take things quite easily; if Rafael did so more successfully, we must not blame him. He was a painter, and his business was to paint. Angelo was a man, and king of men; and his occupation in life was not so simple. He (Angelo) saw Rome for the first time, in 1496: Luther saw it fourteen years after: while Julius II. warred for Bologna, strong in curses and treason, and leagued with the northern vultures, and the League of Cambray: while Angelo sat all day perched on the wonderful scaffold of his own invention, which made his carpenter's fortune, painting the Sistine ceiling, from 1508 to 1511; and while Rafael—a few rooms off—was hard at the frescoes of the inhabited rooms of the Vatican, the Stanze, on which, above all things, his fame will rest and endure. Can you think of those three men together, or so near? Yet, I suppose, the German monk was taken to see the Pope's great painters at their work, and the strange histories of the Old and New Testament, which were now grown nearly all over the Sistine ceiling; and Rafael's stately visions of poets and philosophers submissive to the all-ruling Church; the miracle of Heliodorus, and repulse of Attila. Had Luther talked with the painter on the high scaffold, both their lives, and the face of Europe and the world, might have been changed.

Nothing impresses me much more, as a student of history in a small way, than the advantage of realizing men's possible meetings, and their slight neighbourly knowledge of each other in the every-day-way of acquaintance. It is better than chronology, or mere memory of dates ;—better to remember the period by the men than the men by the period. One has personal interest and imaginative sympathy with the forms and faces of men; and there is no interest in four figures; and it is simply a convenience in getting up a period to begin with the fact that it was somebody's period ; and that he knew and dealt with this, that, and the other person. Yet we must all remember, in realizing the period and life of these great men, that they were not half such great men in their period: a man is no more a prophet in his own time than in his own country. Rafael and Lionardo, and M. Angelo, were not ticketed great or greatest, as they walked about Florence— their work was not done nor approved: their pre-eminence was not settled. Lionardo, the eldest, was the best known and admired, as favourite of the Duke of Milan. Angelo would be talked of as our ex-Medicean sculptor, with a turn for poetry, and a Roman reputation. Rafael probably was described as about the nicest young man ever yet seen in Florence, just like Pico de Mirandola. He must have been commended to clerical patrons, for he seems now to have formed his lasting friendship with Baccio de la Porta, or our Brother Bartholomew, in St. Marco. Think of those two in the cloisters and cortiles, among Angelico's frescoes; perhaps in those days of violent death they could bear well enough to think of the Brother Girolamo Savonarola, lately dragged out of that convent to rack, and fire, and gallows. There is a sheet of paper in the Oxford Rafael Gallery which may be a remembrance of evenings at St. Mark's. It is the well-known No. 28 in Mr. Robinson's book; several heads and hands, and a sketch of the Battle of the Standard. One of these heads is a portrait of Fra Bartolomeo, and he probably sat or stood for another —a very severe and perfect drawing, with hard silver point. This goes back to 1504-5. I could not help anticipating a little, in time; especially as Michael Angelo is one of the representatives of Italian Protestantism, or the earnest and suffering lay-Christianity of religious men in Italy, under the portentous Alexander VI. Florence and Savonarola had prepared him pretty well for what he was to see at Rome of human or subter-human abomination. He did not look on corruption and foul crimes, and the dagger and poison of the Borgia supplementing the sword of St. Peter, with the wide-eyed astonishment and piteous disenchantment of the pious German. Probably he and Rafael made up their minds to see as little as they could, except their art and their models.

We must go back again from Luther's day in Rome, 1510, to the period in Florence, six years before, which brings the two masters together in the lovely city; and brings them also into contact with their elder, the great Lionardo. Most of us are aware that his cartoon of the Battle for the Standard was executed in competition with Michael Angelo and others, to adorn the new Hall of the Great Council, which Bramante, Angelo, and the rest had designed and completed. Only fragments remain either of this work or Angelo's Cartoon of Pisa. The latter in particular is only known, I think, by the old engraving of a part of it, called "The Bathing Soldiers," where a number of men bathing in the Arno, and suddenly called to battle, are struggling hastily into clothes and armour, with an intense expression of wrath and haste which cannot be forgotten by those who have seen it. It has seemed to me that the force of some of those hard faces was put in by the same mind and hand which drew the Fates of the Pitti Palace, described in the Fourth Lecture. Rightly or wrongly, every easel picture of Michael Angelo's is disputed. You hear people say he never painted an oil picture; sometimes that he never painted an easel picture; some of us may remember the angry persistent denials about the recently purchased Entombment in the National Gallery. I don't know exactly what these general statements mean. Do gentlemen really think that he never rested a panel, or canvas, on an easel; or that he never filled a brush with oil colour? What *is* an oil picture? Very often, in the best times, and by the best men—by the Venetians, by Sir Joshua Reynolds, following their methods, and by Turner,— it is a work begun in distemper, that is to say with colours mixed up with size and water,—and finished up with oil colours painted over when dry. I believe that Mr. Watts, who has studied so much in Venice, paints thus to this day; and I dare say Buonarotti combined tempera with oil in his own way. But to reject the Fates as his work; or the marvellous Cleopatra with the asp at her breast, (which some of us must have seen at the Leeds Exhibition, or in London, in 1870, and which, or one like it,

Vasari mentions as Andrea del Sarto's), is to take on oneself the onus of finding somebody else who was more likely to be author of such works. And, as I said, it seems to me that the unfathomable face of Atropos, and that intense loveliness so full of pain and death, was beyond the power of any man who ever painted, save Angelo alone; unless it were Tintoret in after days.

Well, one thing is sure, that Lionardo's cartoon of the Battle of the Standard hung on one wall of the Palazzo del Gran Consiglio, and Michael Angelo's cartoon of Pisa on another; that all the best painters and sculptors in Italy studied them for months, that Rafael studied them among others, and with greater profit than any other; and that they were finally cut to pieces and destroyed unrealized, like several of Rafael's cartoons in after time; so that only fragments of engravings, or more properly engravings of fragments of them, are now in existence. But they were great efforts of the masters' lives; and though there is no doubt that the method of dividing out a man's life and works into epochs or periods may be abused, it is still very useful indeed for the student. The period of the cartoon of Pisa is used by Mr. Robinson in classifying the works of Michael Angelo, now in the Oxford galleries. It is very convenient to dwell on it, because it brings him to Florence again, and into daily contact with Lionardo and Rafael. I have already said something of the advantage of mastering one's chronology by means of grouping great men and works together; and as there is no time now to go through all the biography of either of our heroes, I rather prefer to attempt sketches of times when they were near each other. As yet there can have been no notion of rivalry between them; nor do I think that it was ever bitter or severe: it certainly in after-time amounted to opposition and emulation between the men and their methods alike;—fresco against oil-colour. Their opposition seems rather to have been pressed on by Bramante or others, than to have been the fruit of personal enmity. The story that Buonarotti told Rafael that he went about like a prince with his court, and Rafael told him that he went about like a hangman by himself, proves familiarity rather than dislike. Of that shortly; but at present Michael Angelo was a draughtsman, and a sculptor. Rafael a draughtsman and a painter. Rafael was eight years behind—eight years of such labour and learning as his great contemporary alone could get into the time. He was yet a student, a lad of Perugino's and Pinturicchio's, with much to learn, an endless capacity for learning; and with a style to cast off—not that it was a bad one, but that he had come to the end of it, and other work was prepared for him.* Of Michael Angelo as a student we know nothing: he had no time of unripeness, or crudity, or imperfect handling and progressive work. He went to school to learn, as himself said, to the end of his eighty-ninth year; but nothing is known of Ghirlandajo's, or any one's, claiming to have taught him anything. We hear of him as master; then as Divine Master. And, once for all, do not let us quarrel with Vasari for the word, or undervalue that good fellow. The Boswell of many Johnsons, he was always faithful to his true love and respect for the greatest of them all. He had a great literary and artistic capacity. I believe I may quote Mr. Holman Hunt's opinion of his portrait of Lorenzo de' Medici as a work of the highest order. More, perhaps, than he thought of, may, in truth, and fact, be implied in the word he thus used. For, assuredly, those who knew Michael Angelo from his earliest days did not call him Divine Master till they had seen that God was with him, and that signally.

Next year (1505) Julius II. has been three years Pope; and he, like Mastino della Scala, or Mr. Browning's Bishop of St. Praxead's, orders his

* The Sposalizio, now in the Brera, at Milan, dates 1504.

tomb during his life-time. Michael Angelo's great David has just been set, where it stands now, in the Palazzo Vecchio at Florence. He has done a great St. Matthew;* his marble Bacchus (Uffizi) and the Kneeling Cupid, (now at South Kensington) are remembered; there is no sculptor like him; and Julius sends for him, and bids him design a great mausoleum, with unlimited sculpture. The Slaves in the Louvre, and Boboli Gardens; and the Moses, who now sits gloomily, with bent brows, in the dim lights of St. Pietro in Vincoli, are the finished relics of the master's vast design. Years of his life, apparently the greatest part of years 1516-17-18, had to be wasted in stone-quarrying at Carrara; under quarrels with Julius, and neglect by Leo X., whose Pagan dilettantism had little in common with his spiritual power of design and earnest faith in Christ. At least, he was sadly distracted from his great work; and it was not right to make him a head quarryman. But now, in 1508, Julius does a new thing. His tomb was ordered three years ago, and is little advanced, for he refused to see the master; who thereon refused to stay with him, or work for him; and who altogether took and maintained throughout a very high line, with a very dangerous man. It is

* Academia at Florence.

now settled between them that the tomb shall wait yet longer. The Pope is thinking of the League of Cambray, and the ruin of the semi-Protestant Venice, and has no notion of dying just yet. What he will do is to ornament the Sistine. It was to be a great place of sculpture, all *spirantia signa*, marble life unpainted: but Bramante is the architect of all the Pope's new works, the Loggias, and new chambers of the Vatican. He is of Urbino, and has a brilliant young townsman by the name of Rafael Sanzio, who is painting the new Vatican Stanze in fresco. Both of them are highly popular, magnificent, handsome and so on; and Bramante does not want so much money to go away from his works; and he interferes and protests, in not unreasonable terror of the terrible rival who is architect, sculptor, and engineer already. Is he much of a painter? Bramante hopes not, and persuades the Pope to insist on the Sistine being adorned with paintings. It is Urbino against Florence: rather an intrigue, I am afraid; but a very mild one for the sixteenth century in the Court of Rome. Angelo, the sculptor, with his broken nose, just like an antique, and his mystic piety, and spare ascetic life, and short speech, may be a painter perhaps, Bramante thinks; but with the brush he surely never can come near our young townsman, who has got so much from him and the cartoon of Pisa.

The Florentine sets to work, however; invents his marvellous scaffolding all at once, and mounts it. His design is Titanic. The ceiling shall be a kind of floor of æther, and into it he carries up vast columns in perspective towering into a new heaven. At first he does not understand how to mix his fresco-plaster; and is in despair to see his forms too dim. His first picture; the Deluge, has rather too many and too small figures: by the time it is done he knows his tools and his distance thoroughly. And then men see what he can do—some part of it, at all events. There is his Eve, the loveliest of all forms; there is the Act of Creation; the Maker flying all abroad on the wings of winds; the chain of prophecy from the first Adam to the Second; and between these are vast forms of apostle, prophet, martyr, sibyl, each the shadow of a spirit on the wall. Rafael has something to learn yet of the grim aristocrat: and he learns it, and owns it, with all his frank sweetness, always sure of fame, and joy enough and to spare. I think that this must have been the time when he thanked God that he had been born to know and see the work of Michael Angelo. But he, too, is

changed. What is called the First Period of Rafael *
ends, never to return again, with the paintings of the
four Stanze : that is to say, the "living" rooms of
the Papal Court in the time of Leo X. They are
the Camera della Segnatura, with the Dispute of the
Sacrament, the Parnassus, and the School of Athens;
the Stanza d'Eliodoro, with the repulse of Heliodorus; the Mass of Bolsena for Julius II., and the
Attila and Liberation of St. Peter to suit the taste
of Leo X. Then there is the Stanza dell' Incendio,
or of Charlemagne, containing the burning of the
Borgo, or suburb; and the Sala di Constantino, with
the defeat of Maxentius by the first Christian Emperor: these last being painted entirely by Giulio
Romano, and other pupils, from Rafael's designs;
those of the third room are so in a greater or less
degree. These are his great and central works, extending over his Roman Period, so called: the earlier
part of it, as Mr. Robinson's excellent work puts
it, from 1508 to 1512, and the later to 1517, and
on to his death in 1520. By these, and neither by
Fornarinas, nor by dark-eyed Contadinas as
Madonna di Sisto, nor by red Popes and Cardinals,
—his powers and his faithfulness to them are to be

* His Peruginesque or earliest manner may be said to end with the
Sposalizio, about 1504.

judged. So, in effect, says Sir Joshua Reynolds; I do not know whose judgment ought to prevail against his.

It is admitted on all hands that the influence of Michael Angelo on the mind of Rafael was considerable; but as Mr. Robinson acutely remarks, it was much greater on Giulio Romano and Rafael's pupils. And the fact of their having done so much of Rafael's later frescoes certainly makes the work more Michelangelesque. But if the Sistine and the Stanze were at that time viewed as rival works in fresco, Rafael seems to have left the field to his opponent for the rest of his life; and instead of challenging him any more in fresco, to have pushed on oil painting against fresco. And in the opinion of the Roman public he did so quite victoriously; perhaps it was this which drew out the older man's remark that fresco was work for men, oil painting for women (pray excuse the thoroughly uncivil and improper nature of the observation, but he certainly must have been out of temper at the time). There can be no doubt that fresco, more than any other art-work, calls for the greatest efforts of the greatest man. However, Rafael reigns with Pope, court and people till the day of his death, the other makes designs for Sebastian del Piombo, and tries to get

Venetian colours on his own drawing; as Tintoret actually did in the next century.

Altogether Rafael has the best of it; right or wrong, he is the man of the times, and has gone with the times. He found art the servant of religion, and then he pursued it religiously and did best of all. By the time he had come to the Stanze frescoes, he had made up his mind that art belonged to Apollo, and he went on with it just as cheerfully; who Rafael belonged to, perhaps, he had left off asking. It cannot be doubtful, I think, that when he paints on one wall Christ, as Lord and Chief of the Domain of Theology; and on the other Phœbus Apollo, as Lord of the Domain of Poetry, Art, and Inspiration; he proclaims the separation of religion from art, declaring practically that Rafael painted no longer as servant of Christ, but as a student of classical literature, and as servant of Julius or Leo, those marvellous classical vicars of Christ. All artists had held hitherto, and Angelo held still, that the faith was true, and therefore supplies the highest motives for art. Rafael inaugurated, meaning no harm, the new artistic persuasion, zealously insisted on to this day; that mythologic fable is beautiful, and therefore supplies the highest motives for art. One side said for centuries: truth first, and beauty will follow, and she did follow. The other said: beauty at any rate, and all the world will follow. So they did, and she led them the way of the stranger that flattereth with her words; and art became prostitution, and Italy became a scorn and ruin, a land despised or mourned for, in all places where God and honour reigned.

So Rafael and Michael Angelo went different ways in life, and were separated and opposed in spirit, and partly or wholly jealous of each other. And one died, and the other lived on for the time in Florence; he may have gone there in disgust, leaving Sebastian del Piombo to paint in oil against Rafael. The Raising of Lazarus in the National Gallery is probably one of these compounded pictures. But now in 1520, the year of Rafael's death, the mighty sculptures of the Medici Chapel, in St. Lorenzo in Florence, are begun, for the sepulchres of the brothers of Urbino, nephews of Lorenzo the old Magnificent patron—Giuliano and Lorenzo. How the names were misplaced, so that the bright and fortunate soldier Lorenzo is supposed to be represented by the statue of the gloomy heart-struck Giuliano, is difficult to say, but so it seems to be; the whole subject will be found in vol. ii. of *Grimm's Life.** I have said something

---

* See Miss Bunnett's Translation.

of these before, especially of this statue, called the Thought of Michael Angelo. As an expression of the aim and the power of spiritual art it is perhaps the chief work of the world.

Nine years after, Florence had her last interval of freedom, so they were pleased to call it, for two years (1528-30), and fought hard for her stormy liberty. Savonarola's pupils had been brought up at least to fight for honour and civil life; and her chief artist became her chief engineer, seizing with his sure eye on her strong point of defence, and fortifying San Miniato; having to fly to Venice at last, when all was lost or betrayed. Clement VII. pardoned him at the fall of the Republic, and till 1534 he lived between Florence and Rome, working principally on the tombs of the Laurentine Sacristy. In that year he went to Rome, where he remained till his death in 1564. The Last Judgment of the Sistine was begun in 1534, completed in 1541. The Crucifixion, for Vittoria Colonna, was a work of this period; the tomb of Julius II. was at last completed on a reduced scale, and Moses seated in St. Peter in Vinculis. And his great labours as architect of St. Peter, and the unfinished Deposition in the Duomo at Florence, fill up the measure of one of the lives of highest honour ever won by man.

Immortal honour; I do not know what the words mean, but they belong to the life and death of Michael Angelo; as far as one human creature has right to say them of another at all.

In the Oxford collection there is a drawing of Vittoria Colonna, the one woman whom Michael Angelo loved, who having been wedded once, and widowed, and clinging to her first vows, could not accept his hand, or yet reject his love. It is a noble and delicate face, bearing out what we know of her. In a time of utter licence and universal temptation, when all sins one can or cannot name were matter of pleasure and convenience in Italy, these two lived and met in austere purity of grave affection; heading the Protestant feeling of Italy, dwelling with their Venetian friends on prospects of reform in religion, hoping always for the future of their country, and dying in hope deferred. That I believe is what the rapturous school call frigid. Anyhow there is much honour and faith in it. At all events I greatly prefer frigid purity to vice, hot or cold. Judge of their love by this, that when Vittoria died, the stoical master, who had never complained to man before, broke out in utter lamentation and bitter weeping, and mourned for this especially, that never in life, not till now when she lay dead before him, had he once kissed her hand. I suppose he did it then. For him, when his time came, they laid him in Santa Croce, where Dante should have lain. Πᾶσα γῆ ταφός for them both, as Pericles said of the valiant slain—all earth is their monument.

Rafael, you will see, of course, died in the zenith of his power. Had he lived forty-four years more, like his great rival, one hardly knows what he would have done; unless he had gone to Venice. Had he lived to learn Titian's colour, Velasquez in after days would not have so definitely and absolutely preferred Titian's works as he did. His life is a very perfect one in art, and it was an amiable and harmless one considering his temptations. He, too, was better than his times. But in the records of the mediæval Faith hardly a greater or truer Christian seems to have lived than the aged master, whose last poem willingly declared the vanity of the art which was his glory, and who spoke these dying words to his household:—"In your passage through this life remember the sufferings of Jesus Christ."

LECTURE VI.

DÜRER AND HOLBEIN.

I PREFER cutting our usual bit of descriptive introduction very short this time; and it shall be in better words than any of mine. This is Professor Arnold's contrast between Italy and Germany—for we talk of Northern art to-day:—

> Even thus of old, from the pomp
> Of Italian Milan, the fair
> Flower of marble of white
> Southern palaces;—steps
> Bordered by statues, and walks
> Terraced, and orange bowers
> Heavy with fragrance;—the blond
> German Kaiser full oft
> Long'd himself back to the fields,
> Rivers, and high-roof'd towns
> Of his native Germany.

You can hardly have a briefer or better sketch. But for the real difference between the German and the Italian Renaissance, it is well understood to have been a religious one; and I fear we can only conclude that the presence, the power, and the example of the Popes—and their temporal power on the sunny side the Alps—was the immediate and active cause of the difference. Vital and personal religion in Italy being all on the side of reform, the Papacy stamped out reform; and religious persons had to be satisfied, if they could, with the faith of Alexander VI. and Leo. X.; and with the Holy Sacraments as administered by the commissioned delegates of Alexander VI. and Leo. X.: whatever manner of men they were. So it was, that either the Protestantism of denial, or an indifference too perfect to trouble itself to deny, seems to have gained ground all over Italy; first, after the death of Savonarola in 1498: just as political freedom and civic independence died out, in the subjugation of Florence, in 1530. Michael Angelo, you will remember, left Florence, and the Duke Lorenzo, and Night and Day, for Rome, finally in 1534. He could dwell among the wrecks of Pagan temples, though not with the ruins of the liberty of his own land; and so possessed his soul in patience. But in the North, the German national life, especially that of the free cities, was sturdy and vigorous, cultivated, and often noble. The agricultural population was perhaps worse and worse oppressed by the aristocracy as the central power of the Empire decayed. But the peasants lived on; and gathered strength, and even intelligence, mainly through religious instruction. Germany had never been like Italy in the time of Augustus, and afterwards. She had not fallen under the curse of slave labour, and the degradation and depopulation which surely follows it;—which Julius Cæsar foresaw, and had begun to strive with. Mediæval serfdom, bad as it was, was a far less evil than pagan slavery, and cultivation by Familiæ Rusticæ working in chains. It is impossible to go into this subject now; for it requires a large book to itself: the question, I mean, of how far the early-mediæval weakness and desolation of North Italy was connected with the old Roman system of slave labour. The Imperial divisions of land out in colonies,—no longer colonies of free Roman soldier-farmers, like Northumbrian or Scottish borderers, but systems of slave gangs, without even right of marriage,* without hope of progress, or recognition, or mercy—all this, of course, collapsed instantly on the approach of Ostrogoths or Lombards; because every slave who could lift his hand naturally burnt his master's house and joined the invaders. Probably the cruelties attributed to Alboin were a good deal connected with

* Only "Contubernium."

the revenge of savage slaves on merciless masters. I know not exactly where to direct you for this subject: but between Gibbon,* Mömmsen, Merivale and others, it should be possible to get a competent knowledge of it. At all events it can hardly be disputed that in Italian history civic life, with aristocratic or dynastic rule, are everything: or that in Germany a great rural population existed, which showed its power at the Reformation, moved in the first instance by genuine zeal for the Christian Faith; or that, as Dr. Woltmann says, the Reformation failed in Germany, in as far as it did fail, because the free cities did not stand faithfully enough by the religious protest of the country folk, or second their demands for justice, as under Goetz, of the Iron hand. Then, again, German free cities did not hate each other with Italian bitterness; they had not to look on for generations in helplessness and mutual treachery and hatred, while their broad lands were made the prey and arena of foreigners. It made no difference, as far as real unity or Pan-Italic feeling was concerned, whether Florence were the tributary of the Pope, or the oppressive mistress of Pisa. Political and spiritual hopelessness drove Italians to make their country

* *Decline and Fall*, Ch. ii., p. 42, and especially Milman's *Notes*, pp. 47, 48, ed. 1846.

the library, the museum, the gallery, the music-theatre of Europe, in hopes that she might cease to be the battle-field of Europe. We had better show less self-seeking and narrowness ourselves, before we blame dead men for want of patriotism, or comment complacently on the decay of Italy. Her art and glory are her own: her martyrs to the Faith died also: her distresses really date in their causes from the Social Wars of old Rome; and even from that decay of the Roman or Latin free country-population, which may be said to have begun with Hannibal and Cannæ.

From the novel of *Romola*, and the chapter on Dürer and Salvator, in Vol. v. of *Modern Painters*, an idea of the different moral conditions of Italy and of Germany at the Renaissance may be obtained on the easiest possible terms; that is to say, in the clearest, most graphic, and truest language. We have now to compare the lives of Dürer and Holbein in far different scenes and conditions. Mr. Scott's or Mrs. Hamerton's *Life of Dürer*, and Miss Bunnett's translation of Woltmann's *Holbein*, rest on careful survey of original authorities, and, in fact, are all that can be desired; they refresh their readers and exhaust their subjects, and one can say no more. Let us have a skeleton chronology of the two lives first. Dürer was born in Nuremberg in 1471, and died there in 1528; rich, honoured, henpecked, his work completed—to all Germans the first name in German Art. Holbein was born in Augsburg, as seems after all most probable, in 1495 or '98. His name, however, is identified with Basel, as his father went there early in his life; and his greatest works were done there. He died in 1543 (not in '55, the usual date)—in England, of the plague, which seems to have visited London at shorter intervals, and with more implacable virulence, than any other capital of Europe. And his is the greatest German name in Art, as Dürer's is the chief name in German Art. The leading divisions or epochs of both lives seem to be as follows:— Dürer was married to Agnes Frey in 1494 (Michael Angelo was just flying from Florence with Piero de' Medici, and Rafael went to school with Perugino next year). From November, 1486, he had been learning to paint with Wohlgemuth, of Nuremberg. His father, goldsmith and designer, must have previously taught him to draw, model, and engrave—and he had made a very good Seven Stations of the Cross at home. Three years with Wohlgemuth, four years of Wanderjahre, make 1486-7 into 1493; and he was married as soon as he returned from his first travels. There is no time to discuss Agnes Frey: she was rather hard in money matters, and strict in mind, if she had any mind. But Pirkheimer, Dürer's great friend and patron, and her great opponent, seems to have been as much too joyous in his notions, as she was too severe. Mr. Scott says, with much contempt, that she was of the stuff that saints are made of: which indicates anxiety on his part to show that he does not think much of saints. Perhaps he is used to Scottish saints, as his notion of them is evidently founded on Agnes Frey's characteristics of painful strictness in religious duty and "close grip of the siller." The fact is that Dürer and she were poor up to 1506: that after that date he made money fast, but spent it continually in purchases of pretty things and curiosities, for which his taste was insatiable: also, he was the victim of continual piracies and imitations of his copperplates by Marc Antonio and others, and was too patient and easy with his many debtors. This he himself avows and laments—and I daresay his wife lamented it too—in what terms can never be known, and perhaps it is better so. Born '71, married '94, was in Venice in 1506, after which year the tide of fortune fairly turned in his favour, twenty years before Holbein went to England—the year of Columbus's death. Up to this

(I quote from Mr. Scott's list) his chief paintings are his father's, his own and his brother's portraits, now in Munich; the multitudinous Calvary now in Florence—a pictorial history indeed, where, as German painters were wont to do, he takes the historian's privilege, and repeats figures and events on the same canvas—and a votive picture for Pirkheimer on the death of his wife Crescentia. His engravings were very numerous already. The woodcut illustrations of the Apocalypse are of this date. The Woman with the Wild Man is supposed to be his earliest work, with the Holy Family and the Butterfly—these are, in part, reproductions of Martin Schongauer, or Schön Martin, Handsome Martin—who, as Mr. Scott says, was virtually Dürer's master. The Shield with Death's Head, Adam and Eve, Satyr's Family, Little and Great White Horse, and Holy Family date from 1504—1506. How different a style of Art was in full action at Florence; where Lionardo was drawing the Battle of the Standard, and Michael Angelo the cartoon of Pisa, with that pretty lad from Urbino watching their hands.

At Venice, in 1506, Dürer was on terms of friendship with John Bellini, then eighty years of age, who stood up for him in the talks and councils of the painters; and he must have known Carpaccio, then advanced in life; also Marco Basaiti, Giorgione, and Titian. His letters are chiefly about Pirkheimer's affairs, his loves and commissions: jewels and carpets are to be bought, and Dürer trades as well as he can—his great Altar-piece is a success, and all his pictures sold but one. Some of the painters hate him, he is warned not to eat or drink with them, and they all say his works are very unlike the antique (not a doubt of it). He has misfortunes—his bales of cloth are burnt in a fire—a debtor runs away with eight of his hard-won ducats, &c.: in short, he came back to Nuremberg decidedly a sadder man, and not much richer—grieved to lose the sun of Venice, and not much pleased to meet Mrs. Dürer, I fear. But after this time, his engravings, like Nuremberg's hand, go through every land, and he grows rich in spite of fraudulent debtors and artist-thieves. When a man is worth piracy and forgery, to a person of Marc Antonio's acknowledged powers and skill—he must infallibly get something himself; and Dürer henceforth got enough, and was well content. For his rights, he did not care for them; his charity "sought not her own." In 1509 he begins to write poetry; rough, simple, and wise, with a piety both mystical and practical, dwelling like Michael Angelo on the Divinity and Sufferings of Christ for Man; desiring suffering and endurance for himself; and giving grave, moderate advice for life, like George Herbert's Temple. Mr. Scott has translated some of it so very well, as to enable me quite to get over his remark about saints. Next year Luther is in Rome.

And now we come to the period of the greatest designs on copper; either of religious tendency, as St. Hubert and the two St. Jeromes, or allegorical, like Melancholy and the Knight and Death, dated 1513, the Flodden year. The meaning of the first will probably never be settled. Some say it is the end of the strong wicked man, just overtaken by Death and Sin, whom he has served on earth; it is said that the tuft on the lance indicates his murderous character, being of such unusual size; you know the use of that appendage was to prevent blood running down from the spear-head to the hands. They also think the object under the horse's off-hind foot is a snare, into which the old oppressor is to fall instantly. The expression of the faces may be taken either way: both good men and bad may have hard regular features; and both good men and bad would set their teeth grimly on seeing Death with the sands of their life run out. Some say they think the expression of Death gentle, or only admonitory, as the author of *Sintram;* and I have to thank the authoress of the *Heir of Redcliffe* for showing me a fine impression of the plate, where Death certainly had a not ungentle countenance, snakes and all. I think the shouldered lance and quiet firm seat on horseback, with gentle bearing on the curb-bit, indicate grave resolution in the rider, and that a robber knight would have had his lance in rest: then there is the leafy crown on the horse's head; and the horse and dog alike move on so quietly, that I am inclined to hope the best for the Ritter. The Melancholy is one of the most characteristic efforts of the Gothic mind to express its meditations on its own activity and its end. Her other name is Reflection, or modern self-analysis. As yet she labours in hope: "in the sciences, in mathematics, in hand-work, in architecture: the bell is there to call to labour, the child beginning its labours with budding wings that must grow yet for many a day — the wolf-hound, for the loving service of the brute creation; and the Mistress of all, lost in thought; regardless of the price of all her gains, but crowned with fresh herbage, and with the rainbow of hope before her;"—that is Dürer's allegory of the Vanity of Human Inventions.

In 1515-16-17-18 he was at Augsburg, working for

the Emperor Maximilian, who died in January, 1519 —always Dürer's careful and honouring, almost loving friend—and Dürer determined to go to the Netherlands, where Charles V. was to hold court at Antwerp. The year before, 1518, the Indulgences had been sold in Wittenburg, and Luther's voice had been heard. And in two years more, during which Dürer has been in Holland and Belgium conferring with Erasmus and Quinter Matsys, living en prince, giving and receiving endless presents, and filling his great insatiable eyes with all manner of sights, there comes this sudden outbreak in his journal—there is fire in the gentlest of mankind. One can fancy the wrath of the burghers of Antwerp; they would soon have graver cause for anger, and show it too.

"On Friday (after or before) Pentecost, 1521, comes a tale to Antwerp that they had captured Martin Luther traitorously. The Emperor Charles's herald was given him with safe conduct. On his journey, in an unfriendly place, he said 'he dared no more be with him,' and rode from him. Then were there ten horse (report had exactly doubled the real number) who carried away traitorously the pious man, enlightened with the Holy Ghost, and who was a follower of the true Christian belief, and whether he still lives, or whether they have murdered him,

I wot not. If he has suffered, it is for the Christian truth against the unchristian papacy, which works against the freedom of Christ, exacting from us our blood and sweat, whereby to feed itself in idleness while the people famish. It is very sad and heavy to me that God allows so much false teaching and blindness in men we call fathers, and permits the excellent worth of religion to be falsified and removed"—then follow prayers of exceeding earnestness and beauty, which I cannot read now. Then he goes on, "And so this man, who has written more clearly than any other for 140 years, to whom Thou hast given a spirit so evangelic, being gone, raise us up another who will be able to gather all the world into the faith, and bring Turks, Pagans, Indians, within the Christian fold. O Erasmus, of Rotterdam, where wilt thou dwell? Knight of Christ, ride by His side, thou mayest yet win the martyr's crown." . . . Ah me, scarcely Erasmus. As we know, it was all quite unnecessary; Luther's captivity was a prearranged matter among his friends, Frederick of Thun, and others, and had been determined on by them at Worms as his best chance of safety. The secret must have been well kept. But the passage is an important one in art-history. For Dürer has always been looked on as a representative German;

much more so than Erasmus, and as much so as Luther; and this passage shows not only how deeply his whole nature was moved, but how fixed, and powerful, and far above all other thoughts of his heart, was his personal Christianity. This is German Protestantism, and this is Protestantism in its right sense, or in its positive sense. In the literal sense of the word, as we all see, it is a negative term, meaning inability to hold a doctrine, or conviction of its falsehood: a man's Protestantism in this sense means what he does not believe. But the real use of the word is for strict personal belief in the Second Person of the Trinity. One may certainly think that Dürer's prayers, founded on mistaken news, utterly vain as to immediate fulfilment, were granted in the end; one may see how the notion of violent death in witness to the faith was already before the eyes of thinking men: and if Erasmus's heart failed him, Luther's did not.*

Erasmus sat to Dürer, Quintin Matsys, and Holbein, living in their circle, and as their friend. Those who compare his face with Luther's will see something of the value of portraiture to History. And this seems the best place for me

* See Froude's *History of England*, vol. vi., p. 353: description of the death of Cardmaker, prebendary of Wells, from Foxe, vol vii.

to call attention to two highly characteristic comparisons—that between the faces of the Reformers Erasmus and Luther, and the painters, Dürer and Holbein. Luther and Holbein are all hearty German animalism; theirs are powerful and trustworthy faces: Dürer's is the perfection of manly beauty, with the idealist eyes of inner vision—Erasmus's refined lineaments are certainly such as to give occasion to Luther to say, after their quarrel, and Erasmus's treatise on Free-will against him, that the picture was like the man, full of craft and malice. "A comment," said the late Sir James Stephen, "on the countenance of that illustrious scholar," as depicted by Holbein, "from which it is impossible altogether to dissent."

For Dürer's return to Nuremberg, with his vast accumulation of curiosities and pretty things, Mr. Scott's book ought to be consulted; also for the best rapid description of the beloved old Franconian city; for a sketch of his hero's contemporaries, and two capital etchings of his house, still standing quite as in his days, opposite the Thiergarten Thor. Nuremberg may be reached easily in less than thirty hours from London. It struck me forcibly, during a visit there last June, how very advantageous to a student of German history, or to an artist (and all artists ought to know something of German history) a visit

to that city must be. For with ever so little
preliminary reading : with ever so shadowy notions
about Gothic architecture ; with but a little of the
artist's eye of external interest alone—you can
see the Middle Age civic life just as it was. No
modernized houses are allowed within the walls ; and
the walls are entire all round. You can mount the
Castle Tower and look across the wide rich plain,
and know that Gustavus Adolphus did so morning
after morning in 1632, watching Wallenstein's leaguer.
Red sandstone walls and tiles, and green trees, make
rich music of colour for you ; the Pegnitz goes
racing through the town, muddy and over-hasty, like
modern life ; and modern life gains upon the town
very little more than the Pegnitz. There are the two
"sides," St. Sebald's and St. Lorenz's ; with their two
great churches; the same steep roofs and steep
streets, and bold projecting dormer windows and
massy stone porte-cochères—and much the same sort
of men, horses, and carts, clattering, shouting and
whip-cracking from under them. The Fair Fountain
is there ; it was there in Dürer's day, Peter Vischer's
great work ; Adam Krafft's Sacraments-Häuslein
(the ambry for the Consecrated Elements) was just
finished; and there it stands in the Lorenz-Kirche ;
Veit Stoss's wood-carving is everywhere ; Cranach's

and Wohlgemuth's, and Handsome Martin's works, and one unmistakeable painting of Dürer's own, are all within shot of each other. But when you have had your fill of artistic and antiquarian enjoyment, and are quite full of contempt for the modern time, then go to the Rath-haus, or at present to the Laufer-Thor, and ask the cheery old woman, who lives there, to show you the Burghers' Folter-Kammer, the torture-chambers and dungeons under the walls, and the Iron Maiden. Then you will understand that the discipline of those days, if wholesome, was secret and severe; that burghers had racks as well as nobles, and were capable of abuse in private quarrel; and of revenge, such as neither individuals nor society would take now. Men were reckless then, and took life and death freely; they were not sordid and cruel by greed as we are; but, for all that, their anger was fierce and their wrath was cruel. And Nuremburghers were the best and most ingenious burghers in Germany; but they had their prisoners in cells under the walls and moat, whom no man dared to ask after; and they showed their ingenuity in dealing with those prisoners by the choice piece of smith-work, called the Iron Maiden.

It is an irregularly triangular iron box, like a large fiddle-case: outside it is roughly moulded and painted, with the round face, stomacher, and long skirts of a damsel of Nuremberg. It opens straight down the front, and there is just space for the figure of a bound man to be placed against the iron back inside. Then the doors were shut on him with the aid of a powerful windlass, " langsam, Herr, sehr langsam "— "very slowly indeed," said the old lady above mentioned, with intense sensational enjoyment—and there are eleven long spikes on these doors, which all riddled the poor wretch at once, two in particular piercing his eyes—*langsam*. When he was done with, the Maiden's doors opened again, and also a trap-door at her feet, into a deep oubliette full of water. The frontal and upper bones of two or three crania were produced, found there recently; the Maiden had kissed or crunched off the face and lower skull. I could not make out when she was last used; but it struck me that her abolition, and that of the various infernal machines which dwelt in her company (all worn with use), was an improvement which ought to be credited to these sad times.

There, at Nuremberg, Dürer died, beloved of all men, in 1528: the Emperor Max had ennobled him; he had lived generously, if not extravagantly; he was still a rich man; his work was done early and with great honour: with greater moral dignity, more love and deep respect than Rafael's. Their friendship, as craftsmen, is well known; and how the Italian sent the German a drawing "to show him his hand," and received engravings in return. I hope he did not hand them over to Marc-Antonio.

As great a man as either was living between Augsburg and Basel, and now and then at Ulm. Hans Holbein, the younger, has been trained by Hans Holbein, the elder, in oil painting, and wood engraving, more particularly, since his birth in 1495 or '98: he has had work in the Emperor's Palace, at Augsburg, he has illustrated a Bible in such style as has not been seen either North or South of the Alps; he has been at Lucerne, perhaps as far as Milan; and has been much impressed with Mantegna, and more with Lionardo; he has done endless designs for silver, iron and wood; he has painted Erasmus's portrait, and illustrated the Praise of Folly; his woodcuts are seconding Luther, and flying from town to town, by every city and spire in the wide wide German land. And at Basle he has painted a Dance of Death, in fresco, and has done it again in woodcut:—such a strong terrible unquailing proclamation that death has his day for all of us, and is to be met valiantly, as has not been heard before. The year before Dürer's death, Holbein goes to England—returns to Basle in 1529, the great and grievous Iconoclastic year, when all the churches were stripped—and to England in 1532, where he remained till his death in 1543 (the year after James V. had died of Solway Moss), except for a short visit to Brussels and the Low Countries. He was and is the strongest portrait-painter in the North. Dürer and Holbein must have met or been near each other, but it is not on record that they were acquainted, that I know of. And their difference is this, as artists—Dürer is the last man of the German Middle Ages—profoundly German— of the mediæval spirit, yet full of the new love of beauty; Holbein is as markedly modern. He is Teutonic-modern, not classical or imitative; he is Hans Holbein, son of Hans Holbein, and there is no such other man; but the modern spirit is his; Michael Angelo is as great in a higher way, but in an absolutely different way. The Renaissance which Holbein represents is the new birth of fresh seeking, of new thought, of newly inspired appeal to Nature, of faith in Nature and determination to prevail with her, and win both beauty and blessing from her. In him, as in Angelo, it is religious, because both of them were capable of spiritual thought and aspiration. In many painters it is thirst for beauty only: and their fall is prepared for them. In men of science it is simple activity of mind on their study, or determination to turn the light of their reason conscientiously, and as far as ever it will go, on all things connected with their study, and to prove all things. This spirit was methodized and reduced to rule through Bacon, and the inductive Philosophy; and it has gone on and striven ever since, we partly know how. The study of nature could hold by the Aristotelian limits and barriers of thought no longer. At the end of the Middle Ages, as Professor Maurice pithily says, "men saw that the popes were governed by the doctors, and the doctors by the categories" of Aristotle — by his classification of all things for logical purposes. And men rose up and said, We, and a number of things on which we will have truth, if God will, are not rightly provided for in the categories; and we will have new arrangements for new phenomena. Let us look at facts; at the facts of old; principally at the Greek language, and its literature, and the remnants of its art: and at the present facts of nature, what God has given us to see and to know on Earth of Earth. In an evil hour Theology was set, for base worldly reasons, against all this, and the quarrel has never been healed. But many men are beginning to see that Theology and Science, as things of the many-sided mind, have their mutual limits, and really are not opposed to each other; and their dispute is, I trust, settling into a general boundary question; so far adjusted by this time, that rival professors own to each other that physical experiment and spiritual experience are both, after all, real things: and when that is granted, firm ground is reached.

Now as Michael Angelo is the great Idealist of Modern or re-born art, so Holbein is its great Realist or Naturalist. Both desired truth first, beauty afterwards: but the Italian's longing was for spiritual truth, discerned with the eye of the imagination; the German's gift and nature was to see and draw visible things as they are. He has seen death; and the Dead Christ upon the Cross is drawn unflinchingly from the death, not only with purpose to proclaim His submission to death (which is the real intention of the Crucifix):—but because Hans Holbein saw every sad detail and token of departed life in some corpse laid before him, and it was his duty and necessity to paint what he saw. "Know we not death, the outward signs?" He has seen rude evil faces of dull insult—and the soldiers mocking our Lord are terrible in their uncomprehending everyday cruelty. They are like Hogarth—and Holbein is so, very often in his rougher or grosser faces.

Vice puts nearly the same mark on men's faces at all times.

There are two great excellences, however, which distinguish the noble German or Northern spirit of Holbein from the men of the Renaissance in Italy: that is to say, from the second-rates, like Cellini or Salvator, who fell in with its irreligion and license in reckless despair; or from Giulio Romano, and the classicists, and their academic arrogance. There is neither pride in his portraits, nor sensuality in any of his work. What he sees, he paints, but he insinuates no evil: he did not look for it or think of it himself. Dance of Death or Praise of Folly, or hard, well-drawn protest against indulgences, or broad fun of grotesque, or portrait of lady, or noble, or scholar: there is the right drawing which he learnt for himself untaught, the colour of the best Northern colourist, the weight of meaning, the strong character in touch and line, and lineament; and the grace and rightness which asserts itself against grotesqueness, even in such woodcuts as the Expulsion from Paradise, where death sports before the fallen pair.

His works divide themselves into allegories and histories, chiefly religious—and portrait: the two first, generally speaking, were the work of his earlier days, at home in Augsburg, or Basel; the latter employed him continually in England. There is a capital letter from Erasmus (most of us have read it, I believe), of advice to Holbein, how to behave in England: and I have no doubt he followed it. Erasmus's general opinion of English people is favourable : the rich are highly cultivated, and particularly good to strangers, though he admits the lower classes are very rough. Yet, he says, they are just, and want no more than is due. The great pride of the whole race he speaks of as an essential part of its character; yet, he says, they have reason to be proud. In short, his Teutonic tastes were well satisfied here: with Sir Thomas More and his household, before the evil days of persecution and shaking of nations, while More was Chancellor, and first man of letters in England, while Henry VIII. was yet the delight of the whole land, with the Brandon and Wyatt by his side, and all his mighty men who loved him—the scholar of Basel saw the bright side of England. But it is curious to notice how very different the feelings of Frenchmen or Italians (always excepting Venetians) seem to have been towards this country, whether they came here or we went there. Our Italian proverb of the Tudor age, above quoted, expresses a good deal. "Inglese Italianato e un diavolo incarnato." One custom Erasmus delights in: it is, he says, a nie genug gepriesene Sitte—a habit never enough to be praised. It is the allowed indulgence in that manner and custom, which is proverbially said, in the West of England, to be out of season when the gorse is out of bloom (that is to say, never). English women, he says, are not only very pretty, but very good; and you are not only allowed, but expected, to kiss any acquaintance on meeting her, and parting from her. He probably meant this for a caution, as well as encouragement, to his favourite painter. These are a few lines of Morris's about a yet more ancient England, which must come in here—

> Forget six counties overhung with smoke,
> Forget the snorting steam, and piston stroke;
> Forget the spreading of the hideous town,
> Think only of the pack-horse on the down,
> And dream of London, small and white and clean,
> The clear Thames border'd by its gardens green:
> Think, that below bridge the green lapping waves
> Smite some few keels that bear Levantine staves,
> Cut from the yew-wood on the burnt-up hill,
> And pointed jars that Greek hands toiled to fill,
> And treasured scanty spice from some far sea;
> Florence gold cloth and Ypres napery,
> And cloth of Bruges, and hogsheads from Guienne,
> While nigh the thronged wharf Geoffrey Chaucer's pen
> Moves over bills of lading, &c., &c.

Holbein's Dance of Death is connected in our minds with the cloister wall at Basel, the opposite street to which is still called Todtentanz. But it is doubtful if he ever did paint on that wall—the old

Klingenthal Dance of the Dead was there before him. It is the wonderful series of woodcuts of Holbein's drawing which really will carry down his name for ever in connection with the contrast of Death and Life. A great name is associated with him in it, that of Lutzelburger, the admirable form-schneider or woodcutter. I cannot stop to praise him as he deserves; but the fourth number of *Fors Clavigera* contains, not a woodcut of his hand, but a copy or facsimile utterly undistinguishable from an original print, and due to the exceeding skill of Mr. Burgess. It is the Expulsion from Paradise, Death rejoicing over his prey. And, as our space is limited, we must spend the rest of it on considerations of this and Holbein's other religious or semi-religious works, and of his portraits, German and chiefly English.

You probably will not remember that I made mention of the block-books of the later Middle Ages in my fourth lecture, noting the difference between their way of printing text and illustrations altogether, in woodcut stereotype, like a picture; and the later improvement of movable types, separate letters, which were interchangeable, and could be used for any other text. Well, as writing was derived from hieroglyphics or pictures, so printing went through an analogous process, and the movable types or letters were derived from the earliest rough wooden blocks of illustrative pictures. Wood engraving began, I believe, with playing cards,* and other cards, calendars, &c. Of course, it soon began to be applied to letters and books. Now, the great social importance of printing was, of course, the overpowering numbers in which copies of a new thought or idea could thus be circulated. There was no keeping out the vernacular Bibles; and still less such powerful comments on them as the Indulgence-mongers or the Lamp of Truth. They carried their meaning with a glance, and it went deep, and never came away. Erasmus and Hutten chastised the Pope with whips, but these prints were scorpions. Every sinful man who looked at the Indulgence-Shop for five minutes, would know that German men therein protested to him that he might repent himself for himself to Christ, since Christ gave him the desire to repent; and that that was better than buying pardon in the market of monks, who would let poor men die under sin because they could not pay for salvation.†

* In the conventual use of playing cards, says Dr. Woltman, the court cards were eminent saints.

† The True Light is thought to contain even a portrait of Erasmus among the blinded clergy. He had by this time turned against the Reformation. (Date of Woodcut, 1524).

This is the power of Picture; the whole chain of thought, all that is meant by the Doctrine or Teaching of Individual Repentance, flashed on a man at once. So also with the Dance of Death. In another paper, I said that the most important Triumph of Death of the earlier days is that by Orgagna, at Pisa. Like that great work, Holbein's Dance of Death, or of the Dead, is accompanied by a foreshowing of the Judgment of Mankind. And I think I hinted that the Florentine took a severer and more despairing view of the consummation of all things than the Augsburger. In the Pisan fresco, Hell has the better, in short, and few are saved: in the last of Holbein's woodcuts, the just alone stand before their Lord rejoicing. Yet all throughout warning is given, by threatening text on text, that the sinner risks dying in his sins, unless he repents. "What will ye do in the end thereof?—Gedenk das End—Memorare novissima"—is the all-embracing motto of the work. But there is a tone of half-humorous reflection throughout, on the grand Equality of Death. It is not spiteful or envious: the poor pedlar, with his heavy pack, is hurried off by Death as pitilessly, and goes as unwillingly, as the stern old noble who turns on the Destroyer, and does fierce unavailing battle. Indeed, in some of the later verses, which are supposed rightly to express the painter's mind, Death says only to his valiant victim, "Come thou with me, good sword." But go we all must, quoth the painter, and each will go from his daily life, from ploughing or grinding at the mill; and undoubtedly, ye shall go from the midst of your sins, if ye will practise them. O, king and emperor, cardinal and pope, queen, ploughman, burgher, soldier, old crone and little child, painter, scholar, apothecary, ploughboy, thief, and all-privileged Fool—you must depart for good or evil. Therefore—what? Do not, as Orgagna says, turn hermits and live on hind's milk; but do justly, love mercy, walk humbly in Christ's name; and, above all, fear not. It is not all Christian, this mood of Holbein's—there is in it the Northern death-defiance, and the spirit which greeted the last enemy like an earthly foeman, with scornful welcome; meeting him as Antar the Arab met his enemies;—"even as the ground receives the first of the rain."

The Virgin, with Lily of the Valley, and St. Sebastian are of Holbein's earlier time in Basel. Of the great Passion and the Apocalypse, and, finally, of Samuel and Saul, Rehoboam and the Town-hall paintings, I have one or two specimens here. Realism, character, the mind of one who saw and marked every action, great and small, with the inner eye; Scripture in symbol, according to Hans Holbein—such it is for ever. And his grand industry in all decorative metal-work — clocks, hilts, scabbards, lamps—every variety of really noble and original cinque-cento, that too must pass us by. For his portraiture, it begins for us with his early sketch-books in Augsburg. Kaiser Max; Kunz of the Roses, his fighting jester, one of the brightest, most shrewd and valiant of men; Jacob Fugger, first head of that great house—and others without end—all are very rapid and in hard point lines—the men are written down at once, and there we have them. Dr. Woltman gives all these and more.

Among the endless English portraits; we have, most of us, heard of the first portrait of Sir Thomas More, and that of Archbishop Wareham: of the family piece of Sir Thomas More, Margaret Roper and others, which Dr. Woltman says is a good copy; of Cromwell, the Malleus Monachorum, at Wilton House; of the Whitehall portrait of Anne Boleyn; of Henry VIII., and Jane Seymour.* But the number of indifferent copies which pass for Holbein's in

* Dr. Woltman gives a woodcut from a wall-painting, of Henry VII. and Henry VIII.; a stranger contrast in appearance, as it seems, than any other father and son who ever were represented together before or since.

England is even greater than their number anywhere else; not only are Flemish and even Italian portraits referred to him; but his portrait of Morett at Dresden is attributed to Lionardo da Vinci; and so on. One of these copies remains in Oxford; perhaps from the woodcut, perhaps from the original portrait, of Sir Thomas Wyatt; and it has made an impression on me, not from its merit as a painting, for it has none; but from the likeness which it still preserves to the woodcut, and, therefore, to the subject. Sir Thomas Wyatt was one of the most brilliant men of the time —soldier and poet—and he seems to have made himself popular, and to have died in his prime, when all men loved to look on him, and when his gallantry and beauty were really a pleasure to all people. His and his master's early popularity stood much on their grandeur of appearance, and also on their always being to be seen by all men. They had none of the Eastern pride of state in solitude; they headed every national pageant; they were, in short, fit to be seen like Greeks; the sight of them pleased the people, and they knew it. Wyatt certainly is this: it is wonderful how his face tells the tale of Tudor rule. Its pride is very great indeed; yet it is high and keen rather than unamiable: it is not evil pride, conviction of his own superiority, but expression of the accustomed and ripened habit of command: the look of strongest among the strong. The eye is wide opened and thoughtful; not incapable of tenderness, but totally unaccustomed to be lowered before any earthly man or thing. He looks on all men, not in bravado; but being what he is, he has right, and he knows that none should take offence if his long eye takes note of them: most men he has seen think his look does them honour. And his pride will go lightly through rough work; he is the sort of fellow to pull and draw with the men; he is like his master, and can draw a bow with any man in the Life Guards: his neck was evidently, by the portrait, a mass of sinews, and his muscular strength tremendous. In short, his haughtiness is not dull, but capable of sympathy, at least with all stout fellows; and his own race feel, about him and his like, that Rome may bear the pride of those of whom herself is proud.

Those who compare this face, and the many others of which it is a type,* with the Spanish ideal of Alva—the face of unsympathizing pride—may gather some idea of the power of English aristocracy in its palmy time, and of what it stood on; and of why its influence has survived so many years. While that

---

* There are some good examples of ancient English faces in Millais' illustrations to Tennyson,—" The Sleeping Palace."

sort of man survives in any line of life, and has a fair start, forward he will be, for good or evil; generally for the former. When there are none such, or not enough of them, then—times are come I do not desire to see.*

* Compare the following most important and concentrated passage from Müller, *Chips*, vol. iii. pp. 20-22, "German Literature:"—

"It is only among the lower clergy that we find the traces of genuine Christian piety and intellectual activity;—branded by obese prelates and obtuse magistrates as mysticism and heresy. The orders of Franciscans and Dominicans, founded 1208 and 1215, and intended to act as church spies and confessors, began to fraternize, in many parts of Germany, with the people against the higher clergy. The people were hungry and thirsty after religious teaching. They had been systematically starved, or fed with stones. Part of the Bible had been translated for the people, but what Ulfilas was free to do in the fourth century was condemned by the prelates assembled at the Synod of Trier in 1231. Nor were the sermons of the itinerant friars in towns and villages always to the taste of bishops and abbots. Brother Berthold (died 1272) was a Franciscan. He travelled about the country, and was revered by the people as a saint and prophet. The doctrine he preached, though it was the old teaching of the Apostles, was as new to the peasants who came to hear him, as it had been to the citizens of Athens who came to hear St. Paul. The saying of S. Chrysostom that Christianity had turned many a peasant into a philosopher, came true again in the time of Eckhart (died 1329) and Tauler (1361). Men who called themselves Christians had been taught, and had brought themselves to believe, that to read the writings of the Apostles was a deadly sin. Yet in secret they were yearning after that forbidden Bible. They knew that there were translations; and though those translations had been condemned by Popes and Synods, the people could not resist the temptation of reading them."

LECTURE VII.

LANDSCAPE SKETCHING.

I THINK it may be as well if I go back to-day to one or two observations in former lectures. This is to be a practical one, containing remarks on actual drawing, especially from Nature. And one earlier statement I made was, that doing was better than talking; that on the whole, more art is learnt by copying some beautiful thing from nature than by looking at other men's work—and that till you know how to draw lines accurately, and to lay on tints evenly, you will learn Art best by learning to do so. Therefore, I say to all here, Go and learn to draw something right. You have a good art-school, and may go there to begin with. As soon as you know something of the use of the tools, and of the power and accuracy of your own vision, take up, I should say, Ruskin's *Elements of Drawing from Nature*, and work out his lessons vigorously;

or go to very simple subjects in the open, and do your very best. I do not say this so much to those who are proficients in music, or zealous students of music: though the example of hundreds of men and women will show you that talent is really a blank cheque you can fill up as you like, and that the fineness of nerve which revels in delicate sound will also get and give delight from tender colour. I only say, If you live in, or are being educated for, middle, or lower or upper middle life, life is long enough for you to take up one or both of these accomplishments, or artistic studies, to be the comfort and the help of your spirit while you live. You have time for it, and you will always have time. I have seen with wonder and extreme pleasure, what the hardworking hands of this county can do in music, and I think they have also capacity for the other line of art; and I think that, in all probability, some of them may have natural tendencies to follow it. The fact is, Study of Nature is really necessary to you if you want to get your proper share of the right sort of pleasure in this world; and for the most part you cannot study nature without drawing from nature. Vigorous feeling for art is shown here in the buying of pictures; and the best are generally landscapes: where somebody has gone and bought pictures of what he knew and liked in nature. And the great thing is to vary and extend our study of scenery, and to observe every spring and summer, and all the thunderstorms, or April gleams, and all the sunsets; and, if we can possibly get up, a number of sunrises. (I do not rest too much on this, because it might induce some enthusiasts to omit going to bed at all.) Anyhow, you ought to look on nature as much as you can, in as varied forms as you can, and make your painters do the same. Make them paint your favourite effects; do not encourage them to go on repeating themselves, or their hack subjects, but give a man, if you are able, opportunity and encouragement to do his very best, and do not let him only reiterate the one or two things which he may have made a hit with: if you like a man's work, try and get him to the top of his work—no greater kindness can be done by man to man. Rich people, I think, ought to buy high-priced and large pictures, to prevent the artist's life being quite frittered away with bits, and dots, and splashes, and what are technically called "pot-boilers." It is right to buy what you like, but you ought to like the highest kind of things best—wild scenery as well as home scenery; the dales and the lakes, Switzerland, Scotland, the East, the sea, the clouds, and the ways of the elements in general.

Some allusion was made in my second paper to the account given by Professor Max Müller of the gradual deification of the powers of nature, that is to say, of that comparison between their agency and human agency, through which it may be supposed that some knowledge of personal Deity was drawn from them, with or without help from primal tradition or revelation. The Aryan herdsman, we said, saw natural agency everywhere, in all around him; he felt personal agency going on within him in the will of his heart, and the strength of his hand. He reasoned from his own agency to that of nature, and said, not It thunders, but He thunders; not It rains, but He sends the rain. I said that St. Paul seems to recognize this, since he tells the people of Lystra and Athens that God showed Himself, at least, that He left not Himself without witness, in heathen eyes, by giving them rain and fruitful seasons. We saw that the tendency of the Greek was to go far beyond this acceptance of natural signs of God; and that he made himself gods in his own image—statues, or signs, as Romans called them. Yet, for a time, we said, he did not lose hold of the idea of and hope in One God; seeking Him wrongly, through anthropomorphism or the beauty of man; naming the statues he made Agalmata, or glories, or representations of glory,* Divine and human; things of joy and beauty. And now for ourselves: it has pleased God to refer us to the natural beauty of ravens and lilies, and to the natural signs of rain and fruitful seasons, as His common gifts to righteous and unrighteous: and He drew image after image from natural things; so that it is best for us to consider if, in some real sense which we do not define, these things be not signs of Him, and therefore Agalmata, glories and things to rejoice in. There is no reason for our losing hold of the ancient, natural, and visible evidences of God's working, whereby men felt after Him unknown in old days. We are also to see Him in His works. We are to look on beauty, in the sense of aptitude of structure, as a sign of the mind of a contriver; that is Paley's argument from the watch. We are to look on pure beauty, on colour and form, as signs of the nature of One in whom is all beauty; as Agalmata, and things of glory. And that is the principle, that is the *good*, if there is any good, in English Naturalist Art, principally landscape—that is the good, as distinguished from the pleasure, of our subject of to-day—sketching from Nature. The pleasure men take in forms and colours and their

* ἰφ' οἷς τις ἀγάλλεται, *Hesych:*

manipulation is not the good, but the fun of the thing. I am quite aware that a pious spirit will not make a correct draughtsman, of itself; and there are many undevout men who are good artists, technically speaking, as there have been undevout astronomers who were not mad. And I should say that such men, if they really love their work, will find the time they spend at it the best and loftiest of their life, and that somehow it will do them good. However, we must now talk only of pictures and picture-making, and of that department of it which we call sketching, especially from Nature. Now, what is sketching and what is Nature, in this compound notion?

I suppose sketching means *incomplete* drawing. And what I want you all to agree in at the outset is, that it does not mean imperfect drawing. In as far as a sketch is right, it is perfect so far: in as far as it is wrong, you must treat it as nothing— rub it out, and set it right. To sketch is to set down part of a whole subject on paper rightly;* as its outline and other leading lines. The word is used for making experimental lines and forms to see how you like them—which is merely tentative, and need not be considered here. Again, the word

* Not the whole of a part of a subject, which is a study. See *infra*.

sketch is used, more correctly, for drawing from natural objects, as much as you can in a limited time—the words sketch from Nature being so far different in meaning from the words draw from Nature, that, in using the latter, you imply that you have time to complete your work, and produce a drawing instead of a sketch.

Then for the word Nature, it means things as you see them, in the first instance : only we are to distinguish drawing from Nature from drawing from models or copies. And in that way I suppose Nature means anything which has life or growth in it, anything organic; something which is not done entirely by the hand of man. Neither a drawing from a statue, nor an elevation of a steam-engine can be called drawings from Nature ; they are drawings from the object. A blacking-bottle is an object, a double wallflower growing out of it is Nature; and Tim Linkinwater felt it so, and was affected accordingly.

Then for another word—Study. I suppose a study is a carefully-finished record in form, or colour and form—the whole of some part of a picture, or of a single object — highly finished, perhaps entirely for the sake of the execution. A sketch, as distinguished from a study, will generally mean the completion of a stage of the whole picture, or a part of the whole of it, as a study is the whole of a part. A sketch for a picture will be the lines or light and shade of the whole subject: the study will be the whole or completion of a part of a picture: only, when the rest of the picture is done, it ought to fall into its right place, perhaps an unimportant one. And the greatness of a picture or a painter may be said to depend on his power of giving devoted attention to study of all the parts of his work, keeping them all the while in the proper relation to each other. The strongest man is he who makes you see that he is greatest in great things, without being wrong, or indeed incomplete in anything.

But now we, or some of us, want to go out next spring, and draw in the woods or by the waters, and bring home pretty drawings. Well, the first thing is to be able to draw something right at home. And there are two lines of study, which I think all intending sketchers ought to carry on in your art school. In the first place, freehand and gradation; in the next, study in sepia. Do some careful copies of branches, from Hatton's photographs and the *Liber Studiorum*, as soon as ever you have learnt the broader characteristics—of trees from Harding. First learn the facts of form, and store your mind with characteristics—of trees, suppose, and foliage; and to do this you must draw in chalk or pencil. Then, when you have gained some knowledge to express, take the best instrument to express it: the fullest and the finest, the most rapid and subtle; begin with the water-colour brush at once, as soon as you know forms by heart. And set to work with this purpose, to learn to use the brush as a pencil or drawing instrument. Learn to make sharp triangular cutting touches, and to run them into each other so as to create a form; keep a brush and sepia at hand, and be always creating three or four leaves, or a spray at a distance. Block out a tree form in pencil, and determine with pencil what the outlines of leaves and trunk are to be, till you know what you want to do, or what to do next. Then do it, with the brush.

And here we come to Mulready's celebrated saying, which runs through all art and every operation of art, and is as applicable to Titian painting a Doge as to a pupil-teacher making a study of a cast of blackberries: "Know what you have to do, and do it." The first part comes first, of course. In every sketch and drawing, you must know what you want to do, and also how much you can't do. For want of that many of us are always trying to do, or to get in, too much, and so fail to get anything in quite right. "Know what you have to do;" that is to say, have a leading and well-defined idea, which shall be always the principal idea and feature in your work; let that be central, and let all the parts, as painters call them, all the minor ideas, minister to it.

There is a portrait of Doge Andrea Gritti at Denmark Hill, which you will find partly described in my book,* with reference to this point. It would not matter to Lionardo or to Titian in what order they did their work. Neither would care whether he painted his accessories first, or the face and form of his subject. For both he and Lionardo knew alike what the face and form would be before they painted it; each had the power of conceiving of his picture, and seeing it within his head, as the Laureate says, before he touched the canvas. (Don't forget that expression, as it is the briefest and strongest account of the imaginative gift which you can possibly have.) This is what knowing what you want to do means, or what you have to do. You must be able, and you can in some degree learn, to have a sure and precise and tenacious vision of what the white paper will be like when your drawing is finished on it, and it isn't white any more. It is not so difficult when you have

* *Oxford Art-Manual.* Macmillan, 1868.

Nature or the object before you; because, when you have forgotten your original whole conception in its parts, and in the processes of its execution, you can often look back on the scene you are working from and patch it up again tolerably. But even with a landscape before your eyes in Nature's colours, you must try to know beforehand what it will be on your block, when it is done in the pigments of Messrs. Winsor and Newton.

To be a drawing at all, every drawing must have passed through your brain and be the result of a rapid act of memory. You observe the form of a bough and put it down on your paper, but you must look at the paper and paint from memory so far. And this is the lamentation and mournful tale of all sketchers, that Nature won't wait for them, and changes incessantly; nor only that, but that she changes with a gigantic and terrible rapidity of varying phases of beauty which turns their heads and confounds them altogether. It is so—we shall join in the lament directly. But take this also with you : you must consider your picture before you begin, not only till you have a distinct notion of what you want it to be when finished, but till you have a notion of all its stages, so as to be able to see where you are at every process and stage of your work, near or far from your first intention and thought. For in proportion to your tenacity and faith to your first thought will be the power of your picture, almost to a certainty. This is the secret both in rapid sketches and finished pictures, to have and to be true to a leading idea: as Turner said, to paint one's impression—the mental image of the coming work. These are some lines of Browning's from *Pippa Passes*. The young sculptor speaks; he is a capital fellow, though perhaps a little priggish. He says he

> Bids each conception stand while, trait by trait,
> His hand transfers its lineaments to stone.

that is to say, he is able to *prod* down his leading idea and never lose hold of it, while he does all its accessories, difficult and interesting as they may be. Now, something of this you must be doing in every picture and every part of your picture. Every touch must be a thought or a part of a thought, in theory and almost in practice; and all these parts or minor notions must come at last to be organic parts of the whole, that whole being your finished drawing, the realization of your thought, the record of what your eye and mind have seen. The Duke Lorenzo is called, and most rightly, "the Thought of Michael Angelo." He saw that form in the block of marble, and chipped away till all the world may see it; that was his expression, as all remember, about gradually finding the statue in the block, as he transferred the form to the marble from his brain; where it lay pent, like a spirit in prison, behind the bar of his heavy brows. And he cut the dress and its details with patient precision and minuteness, for joy of the strength that he knew was in him, to make the brooding face and gesture rule every detail. He could make the highest part of his work prevail over all the others, whichever he did first. So could Lionardo : it made no difference to him whether he painted his pebbles in first, or the features of his Virgin; he knew very well which people would look at when his work was done. So with Titian : he paints a gold girdle and bracelet, or a Doge's gold lace, as if he had the soul of a jeweller; but when the face is done, of doge or lady, who can look at anything else before it? The rich dress and ornament minister to the presence and the bearing of the subject, and say, this man or this woman adorned their fine clothes better than their clothes adorned them. Their state would not have become them, but that they themselves were kingly. Or at least Titian would have them so, and conceived of them in their best hour, fixing them down then and thus.

Therefore in sketching, as in all else, the right facts in their right order make up, and are the whole thing. As Swift said of writing, it is true of painting, right words in right places. And you begin a drawing with the outline, because the boundaries or separating lines of its masses of colour are generally the leading facts in it. What you see—now do remember this—is a certain number of patches of colour relieved variously against each other, or blent with each other. What strikes your eye most is the relief of those colours against each other, and you naturally draw lines to represent the boundaries of such relief.

These are outlines. The principle of water-colour is from light to dark. Your high light may be white paper or oxide of zinc. Your dark shades cannot be darker than lamp-black; and in theory the lamp-black touches ought to be put on last, and all the others in gradation of depth. Sky line, principal forms of cloud, middle distance, foreground, and something there to lead into the picture,—all this is expressible by line, and, till you are powerful workmen, all this ought to be faithfully drawn with a hard pencil before you put on any colours at all; that is to say, when you mean to complete a drawing as a composition or record of your observation of

Nature. I say a composition, because a sketch with a leading idea, any combination of ideas expressed in form or colour, anything more than a study of a single object, without backgrounds, is ipso facto a composition. Composition means putting together with object and purpose, and your leading idea is that object and purpose. Rizpah is the leading idea in this mezzotint;* there are plenty of others, but they all centre in and minister to Rizpah and her dead sons. Turner had seen these trees in Yorkshire, most likely; and the sheaves of barley harvest in many lands; and the broad moonrise on many a night, and the leopard at Exeter Change; and the sad mother and her torch within his head. And he brought all the other ideas together to minister to and set off his thought of her. What you care for most in a sketch you must make every one else care for most; that is composition, and it is necessary to every sketch which you intend others to see, as a drawing of anywhere or anything. You may often— and it is the best thing you can do, very commonly— make rapid studies of colour, whose only object is to record that at such and such a time, for instance, on such and such a mountain, there was a glow, which you caught the hue of with carmine and cadmium

* See Plate in Turner's *Liber Studiorum*.

yellow, stippling with carmine again to form, putting rose madder and blue shadows, glazing with chrome when it got too cold, or spotty, &c. In this case the colour is your leading idea, and the principal parts of the picture will be where it is richest, and where you have caught its richness best.

The essence of sketching, you will always and most rightly be told, is character. To say what is that always comes to something like this; if you have to draw a fox and goose, the fox ought to look intensely foxy and the goose intensely goosy, like Mr. Bretton Rivière's three years ago; or if, as Sir Joshua Reynolds said, your subject was a cat or a fiddle, the cat ought to be thoroughly feline and the fiddle should express violinism in general. Character in art means the expression of the inward and special nature of the thing drawn. What Carlyle effects in history is the painter's aim in picture-record,—to give the individuality, the quiddity, as old logicians called it, of his subject. There is something in every man which distinguishes him from all other men; so there is in every rock or tree—at all events, you would not choose either rock or tree to draw if it were not distinguishable from others, and had no quiddity. But for momentary variations of character, for special emotion, the character of a special scene, look at the dog in Cephalus and Procris, all canine sympathy and grief; at the leopard in Rizpah, irresolute, watchful, impatient; at the tree-trunks in Jason, all bristling with horror and suspense; at the ineffable attitude of the Duke Lorenzo. Seize thus on the specialty of everything you draw, and make others see it, and then you have the master in you. Do it in correct form, *i.e.*, light and shade, and you are a master draughtsman. Do it in beautiful colour with correct form, and you are a painter also. But this account of character quite falls in with what we have been saying about a leading idea being necessary to a picture, and the composition of a picture meaning, proper adjustments of all its parts, or minor ideas, to bring out its leading idea. Its leading idea is its character, its smaller ideas are the touches which compound the character, or are composed into it. Character is a Greek word, which means deep marking; it is from χαράσσω, to engrave or plough deeply; harass, I suppose, is from the same root. Where the plough and the harrow have gone over a man there you generally see some lines on his face; that is his χαρακτήρ or character, the writing of his ways on his look, the seal on his forehead, perhaps, of what sort of service he has served. Every man's fate is written on his forehead by the hand of God, Persians say.

And so all things have their histories; and the marks of their histories in themselves are their character or specialty. You have read, or know, about the growth and gradual building up of a tree, and how all his life and trials and accidents and successes record themselves in his fibres as he is built up. That is character; an oak's is different from a birch's; and a park oak's is different from an oak growing out of the rocks by a torrent side. Their features differ according to their position and prosperity, as men's faces differ according to their conditions; only that the oak has not had any moral choice in bringing himself to what he is, and the man has. And it is the instinct and habit of seizing on features, combining them, remembering them, reproducing them, which makes a great poet or painter in its higher grades, and a good sketcher when it is possessed in a moderate degree and faithfully improved.

Now, the lines of the plates in Turner's *Liber Studiorum* are quite visible, and the plates are easily accessible in autotype facsimile: they are his own lines, etched with his own hand on the copper— *i.e.*, drawn freely as he liked on the wax etching-ground with which the copper had been carefully encrusted; and then bitten with nitric acid.

In this lecture, as in others, I have tried to show

you works which really bore the hand of the master himself; and I have made as little use as possible of copies. The trees and foliage of the *Liber Studiorum* may be followed with great advantage. I should recommend everybody who means to sketch next summer (beginners in particular) to draw these or some such forms over and over again. And, indeed, it would be well, as was hinted in the first of these papers, if all who mean to be judges of drawing, all who expect to have to form opinions about Art or decoration, would go through the simple study of form I suggest. To see anything really you must know how to draw something. And I trust you will not be disappointed with this lecture because it goes so much into technical directions for actual drawing, or for preparing to draw from Nature. For Art is τέχνη, and lectures about Art must be technical : it is doing, and not talking; and criticism even of naturalist pictures and landscapes must be based on knowledge of Nature ; and not only an artist, but a physiologist will tell you how essential the study of drawing is to acquiring that. I would, then, whether I meant to study drawing regularly or not, copy some such lines as these. I would first make a tracing in pencil, so as to get a *faint* outline on white paper. Then I would take a softish quill pen with a broad point, set the original, my photograph, or *Liber Studiorum*, before me, and draw the forms, touch for touch and line for line to the hundredth of an inch with brown ink, or feeding my pen with sepia from a brush; not merely inking the faint pencil outline, but using it for guide, and drawing about one-eighth of an inch from it. It is very difficult and tiresome; but you do learn from it, and you learn exactly what the sketcher wants, the power of rapid expression in line. Every hour spent over Turner's trees is so many minutes gained in every hour of open-air sketching; and so much power gained of making rapid memoranda; which are as necessary as drawing from Nature, as laboured studies with unlimited time. Though, N.B., the laboured studies must be made, and made conscientiously, before you can make a pen-and-ink drawing of your own thus in Turner's style. "Turner's style" means putting in all the facts right: and you must aim at this too. You must not only imitate what he did, by copying the *Liber Studiorum*, but you must find out how he did it by copying similar objects in Nature. Copying Rafael, or copying Turner in the best sense is not the same thing as copying a Rafael drawing or a Turner etching. It is not so much making facsimiles of their drawings—though that is necessary—as working from Nature in the way they worked. First see Nature in Turner; you can learn to do so in the *Liber Studiorum* or in some of the many works at South Kensington. Then go out sketching and verifying him; see Turner in Nature; and make notes of her, as he did in the *Liber*, and the early sketches.

As we are all of us too well aware, the great thing in sketching is not to get hurried or bothered; to know always where you are in your picture, and what you really are drawing, at every touch. This is knowing what you want to do, and doing it all through your picture, and keeping before you the original idea of what it is to be; and enough has been said about this before. Of course, if you find —as who does not?—that you lose your head in your work, the only thing is to take a subject with less in it, or take a bit of your subject first. The round central trees in Rizpah, or the Y-shaped trunks in Cephalus and Procris, will give you trouble enough, if you can get every line in your work to answer every line in Turner's; and nothing else will do.

But now, there are sketchers and sketchers; and at this time, as well you know, great advances have been made in technical realization since Turner's time. Portable tents and huts arise; months are spent on Highland moors, or weeks in Swiss glaciers; and a degree of elaborate finish has been reached which is often genuine finish by added fact;—not mere polish or stipple, but thorough working out. You will see the perfection of Turner's finish by reading the illustrated chapter on "Finish," in *Modern Painters*, Vol. III. But there are later masters of true finish whose works are easier to understand, and whose high completion is more obvious. The two surviving Hunts, with Mr. Brett and Mr. Inchbold, seem to me to be the best examples you can study from in this way, especially as all four are brilliant colourists.* And let two or three in a year, at least, of your out-of-door drawings be drawings indeed; that is to say, studies in colour, with plenty of time given them on the spot, and such arrangement for your own comfort on the spot as shall enable you to work at them in comfort; for without comfort at your work, you can't keep up your attention. Rapid outlines you are pretty sure to make; they take no time. The thing is to choose an easy, interesting subject, where you can say in one or two words what the main interest is; something you really like, when you can say why you like it, and know what you want to do. This is its character; and whatever else

* Mr. Goodwin's colour is as correct and instructive as it is vivid.

you do, get this. Rocks in a beck, or a deep pool, or a bay in a lake, or, best of all, a small mountain tarn with a good cliff over it; two or three old houses or sheds with a tree;—something you really like, and little enough of it. Then take it up and work two or three hours a day at it, at the same time of day, till you really can see no more to do. You will not be satisfied, nobody ever is who is worth a rush; but you will have learnt facts and gained strength. We will come to this again. To go back, I said there were sketchers and sketchers, and all draughtsmen from Nature may be divided into two classes—those who naturally look for and see masses, and change, and motion in Nature; and those who look for and see detail and minute structure and delicate form. I say look for and see, because (abused as the saying is) it is quite true that what you look for you will see in Nature. And of course I mean that the man of sweeping lines and masses ought to be able to draw blades of grass and veins of leaves in his foreground in the right degree of elaboration, as Turner did; and also that the man of detail must be able to put in his clouds and distance faithfully, like Brett or Inchbold. I take Mr. Alfred Hunt as nearest the Turner type; and Mr. Holman Hunt stands by himself as almost a martyr to his own intensity of perception, in distance or foreground.

I suppose every sketcher belongs to one or other of these two classes ; and I think, also, if he is pretty high in either class, if he can draw ferns right, or if he can draw clouds right, he has it in his power to do pretty well in the other class also. But the difference between these men in their work is, that ferns will generally wait for you, and the clouds will not. The pre-Rafaelite can elaborate his subject day by day: the Turnerian is driven to imaginative effort, and must fall back on stores of former knowledge of cloud. His mind and memory work harder — the other man's eye works closer. But Turner's own coup d'œil, or capacity for taking an impression of a picture from Nature, and fixing it all on his mind so as to be able to paint it afterwards, seems quite unexampled in the history of art and of mankind. And his memory and knowledge of Nature were so colossal and unfathomable that he could supply the facts of a scene as he went on painting it — and better and truer, and more multitudinous facts than any other man's. He, then, never sacrificed the power of rapid production, and knocked off a drawing full of detailed facts in a couple of hours.

Holman Hunt's wonderful tenacity of purpose,

keenness of eye, and power of hand, enable him to paint very rapidly indeed ; and he really does so. But I think he carries his conscientious feeling about invariably painting everything from the object itself too far, to the loss of valuable time. The Isabel was rapidly painted, though of course elaborately ; but so much time was lost in getting its properties together—in getting a particular flower-pot made for the basil, and in special contrivances to keep that identical basil alive and flourishing while he drew it leaf by leaf, and so on—that the picture was delayed for months ; but, at all events, it was glorious when it was done.

One of the best writers on sketching I know is Mr. Hamerton. The *Painters' Camp*, especially for all who love the North country, too, contains all the detail of preparations for painting from Nature with elaborate comfort—for comfort is necessary to elaboration. And he gives close and detailed description of effects and special scenes, which are admirable examples of notes made in writing to assist sketches in line : that part of his book cannot be read too often. And it is another reason for doing a little real drawing, that close, well-marked description in writing is scarcely possible now, without the painter's eye.

For a regular open-air drawing, you must take to it as you would to any other water-colour drawing. I have only time to speak of water-colour; and besides, while you are still students of form, it is infinitely easier to draw accurate forms with the water-colour brush than with the hog-hair tool. So begin your open-air sketch with a very light coat of yellow ochre to secure your outline, and then run a thin grey over your distance to keep things together. Then paint manfully into that, according to planned form, drawing things as you see them; first, laying their lightest tint all over, then cutting out forms on that by patches of darker hue. Put on everything in a patch of definite form, and let the edges dry without softening off, unless they are evidently wrong, or unless you have good reason. For the strongest painter is he who does most with the edges of water-colour touches or patches, who is always drawing crisp forms with his brush.

But now for your first out-door subject. It should, I said, be something you like well enough to work out à outrance, but which is not overpowering; which has not too much material, and which allows you to work coolly, and not get into a state of emotion or flutter. And I have a fancy myself for something which has calm water and reflections in it to begin with. It makes you draw things twice over without fatigue, both ways up ; and it teaches you to make so many practical observations about reflection. It gives you a leading idea of calm, and a principal feature to enforce it by ; consequently, you almost always find that such a sketch composes itself well. But, of course, those who will draw architecture steadily, and match their colours as they put them on their correct outlines, will gain more distinctly and certainly. One or two of Prout's lithographs should be always at hand in every art-school, and must be copied with real exactness in pencil. If you will take up and work out some of his subjects—pieces of them, I mean—in pencil during the winter, you will be much better able to do architecture on occasion. But, remember, that architecture and trees will change every month or week of the summer, in colour and relations of colours. In spring and summer colour you must do what you can for yourselves. Prout's colouring will not help you much for bright green leaves against delicate grey stone, for instance. And in architecture beware of too heavy shadows : remember that a dark shadow thirty yards off is not so dark as one at ten yards ; and that shadows are gradated as well as lights, or rather that shadows and lights alike are only patches of darker or lighter colour. But the sharpness and correct edge of a dash of pale shadow will often give a picture far more light than black oppositions of darkness.* And here, as a North-countryman by family, connexions, and fancies, let me congratulate you on living within reach of the most characteristically beautiful scenes in the North country. As far as I have seen, there are two places, for town and wilderness, where the beauty of Old England is specially great, and where it is intelligible at a glance; where sentiment, form, and colour strike any beholder at once—Wharfedale and Winchester; the whole spirit of the North country, in two or three miles, and the Saxon and quasi-Arthurian city. It was no wonder that old Turner's heart went so after the shores of Wharfe. No one who has seen them will ever forget them; but they, and the Dales, and Craven were the land he loved best to the day of his death; and he literally wept when he remembered them.

There is another thing in these *Liber Studiorum* sketches—that in all of them the leaves and vegetation are brought so near the eye in the extreme foreground, that they determine with precision the

---

* I think that for strong yellow light, as in harvest fields, brown madder is the hue for foreground shadows.

distance of the figures from the eye. Also observe the lead into the picture in each of them. As in the etching, so in the finished mezzotint, Turner makes you go into and through his work in his way. And see, in Cephalus and Procris, the distance and perspective given, by the way through the wood, in the centre and the interlacing trunks. Little things, perhaps; but they are just the things which one remembers in some sketch of one's own, and when they are put in they make no small difference.

This brings me to Perspective; and I know not what to say about it so near the end of my lecture. Think you are always drawing through a sheet of glass, upon its surface, and that your paper is that sheet. No knowledge of perspective will make a drawing beautiful; but any ignorance of it will put one all wrong: and a gross ignorance of it is ruinous. And I cannot tell you what easily-perceptible mistakes are, or used to be, made, not only by men with great names, but by men who deserved them: mistakes not only visible to good draughtsmen, but which made amateurs feel that something certainly was wrong. All I can say is, learn to draw a square box, and then imagine it in the middle of your paper, whatever you draw, and mind the vanishing points along its imaginary sides. The most common mistakes in perspective are those made in drawing lake shores, which too often awaken in the mind the thought of a willow-pattern plate. But perspective is very necessary in drawing tree forms. Look at the two plates in *Modern Painters*, Vol. V. "The Dryad's Toil" and "The Dryad's Waywardness," they are both of the same bough. Therefore, in all your studies from Nature at home, of boughs and branches of trees, remember to make two drawings of each bough, one sideways, and one end on.

I am still inclined to recommend Harding's Lessons on Trees to those who are just beginning to draw trees, though Turner's are far better: Harding's are easier at first, and he gives you exercise after exercise for the hand, like scales on a piano, and nobody else does. And he gives you such broad characteristics of the different trees, that imitating them must be of great use at first. Do it with brush and sepia, as well as with pencil or chalk, and as soon as you have got some knowledge of the shapes of masses, and character of trunk and boughs in the different trees, go to Turner's lines and to Nature. Harding's typical forms should be practised in large, on a black board or a sheet of cartridge paper; this will teach you to draw from the shoulder. All tree-drawing is a symbolic shorthand; but Turner's, when you have learnt it, is an universal system of it, and should be used alternately with the photographs. I would use tracing paper at first with both—anything for exactness. I wish, and it may yet be possible, that every artschool might be supplied with copies of Turner's simpler coloured works, so accurate as to give a real transferable or translatable idea of his markings and their significance; for that is his power, the amount of meaning in all his lightest touches.

Finally, you will be always making rapid sketches in line on journeys. I have nothing to say against it; but do write down on each something, at least, about the colours you mean to put on; and do try to put some of them on before you have forgotten all, or driven one sketch out of your mind by another. Many very able and conscientious artists are content to go out for an hour or two of sketching and note-taking, and to return home to put on colour, and carry out notes made on the spot, in a finished work. But never let the hastier outlines or maps of scenes gain on you in your sketch-book. Make, if you like, careful complete outlines, pen and ink them over, and keep them as memoranda of facts, or as charts in detail of pictures to be painted. Your sketch-book, properly so called, ought to be filled, not with fully-considered or finished pictures at all, but with faithful notes in form or colour, or rapid memoranda of the lines of natural compositions—memoranda made of things which "come nicely"—as sketchers say. Incompleteness, not imperfection, is the law of sketching, and I hope it will not be a burdensome one to you.

LECTURE VIII.

POETRY OF LANDSCAPE.

WHEN I remember the quite passionate pleasure I used to take in landscape, especially wild mountain scenery, a few years ago, I am surprised at two things—one is that it is so much moderated, yet extended; and the other, that I have so much of it left *post certas hyemes*.

There certainly are phases of mind; one does pass through differing conditions of thought and feeling. I remember that the painter of several of the greatest sacred pictures which ever were painted, Mr. Holman Hunt, said to me years ago, "I cannot paint any more sacred subjects: people ask me why I don't do a Light of the World every year, and I can only say, it would not come out of my heart now in the same way; the phase of mind for that work is past. I can't repeat it for money." And Mr. Millais, also, as well as Mr. Dante Rossetti, paint no more definitely religious subject. I do not admit the "Moses, Aaron, and Hor" into the category of sacred subjects; it is a wonderful study of two old men, one of them twice repeated—an aged Hebrew of sedentary habits he seems to have been, and about as like Moses as he is like Fagin. I do not believe these men's feelings or regard for religion or religious work to be any colder. In the first case it was the painter's all-searching conscientiousness which spoke; it was his will not to force himself on sacred work which did not call him from within. And, indeed, men jealous of their own motives, and revering sacred subjects, are scared from it now, by the hideous display of pious pictures, done for the market, which annually stare on us in the Academy. There is a religious market, and pictures painted for it appear to me the very reverse of sacred. Besides, men are led on into the world and its great joys and sorrows; and their early sacred work is like the morning-service of their long day. Perhaps one or other of them may return to it later.

> Be the day weary, or never so long,
> At length it ringeth to evensong.

But nothing can be weaker or worse than attempts to take up sacred work when you are not really called to it. I suppose most men who have any spiritual life or consciousness at all would gladly be called to it with sense of power and talent; but certainly those who are so are few. When I have thought of the possibility, if there ever were one, of myself taking up a sacred subject, I have soon become aware that the feelings I should have pursued it with would not have been sacred in any strict sense. The subjects which occur to one out of Holy Scripture really have for motives some human feeling, or action, or terror, or depend on high landscape. I once used to put down subjects for pictures which I should like to see painted, from the Old Testament in particular. These were one or two. Zebah and Zalmunna, when the son of Gideon could not rise up and slay them, being a youth and tender, and they gravely bade the father do what was needful in his strength—the motive is only grave endurance of death. Or I still wish Mr. Watts or Mr. Armitage would paint the scene on the hot rocks of Adummim, when David longed in his thirst, and said, "Oh that one would bring me water from the well of Bethlehem, that is by the gate;" and when the three mighty ones broke through a host for their master:—but he poured out the water to the Lord. That, is after all, a feat of arms—only it and the next strangely illustrate the character which was after God's own heart. Again, the answer to Abishai, when he asked leave to take off the head of the dog who cursed David. Hath not the Lord said unto him, Curse David? I used to have some vague idea of a sunrise on the hills of Moab (the long crimson line of Abarim), which should realize how the water came by the way of Moab, red as blood in the level Eastern light, at the bidding of Elisha. And I actually did make and exhibit two drawings from Arabia Petræa, after an expedition to Mount Sinai in '62. These are almost the only ideas or impressions, of possible "sacred" pictures that ever passed through my mind; and I should certainly have desired to have such ideas more than any other form of idea. Every one is right in drawing what he sees and most enjoys the sight of, but few men, and those not often in their lives, have the inner vision of sacred history or symbol borne in and presented to them, praying to be painted, so that their desire and delight is to realize it in form and colour.

Now a lecture or two ago I spoke of the asceticism of the early and medieval church as flight into the wilderness from the distress and corruption of ordinary life at the time; and the modern English spirit of landscape painting seems in some sense a modification of this feeling. A Benedictine or Byzantine monk escaped into the cloister, and painted or inlaid saints with gold backgrounds and traditional features partly because he was hopeless in this life, and had hope with the saints; partly because the Lombards admired his work, and spared his throat and his cell in consequence. (I leave out, though it is most material, that, as a further consequence, he was generally able to teach some of them the Faith, or raise them to better thoughts of it.) Angelico fled into St. Mark's and Fiesole, because Bianchi and Neri, Guelphs and Ghibellines, greater arts, smaller arts, and Ciompi, were fighting to death in the streets of Florence, and he had no stomach for civic massacre. Turner fled away into Craven out of Maiden Lane because life was utterly hideous and unlike any divine work on earth in Maiden Lane, and he desired to see and record God's work on earth. A lad of our own day will give up notions of advancement in a trade or profession, or let himself be crowded out of it, because he thinks he can live frugally by painting landscape, and that that will suffice for pleasure in life. These are, or were, all practical ways of giving up life to art or for art: that is to say, in the hope of living humbly by and for it. They are all forms of resigning the ordinary successes of life. In some spiritual motive is pronounced; in others it is latent. A certain sacrifice is undertaken, at our own risk if we have mistaken our call and our powers. So it is with all aims. But in painting it is perhaps truer than in anything else, that the wolf's gallop wins, the long gallop that never tires, the steady day's work through the life-time.

And as the great and chief examples of this preference of Nature before all, we have men like Scott and Wordsworth, born in the purple of the heather and in the gold of gorse and broom, stoutly holding their life the best, before all men, and persuading all men too.

Let us just consider what a very new thing the national taste for landscape is; for it affects wild landscape in particular.

Nobody really cared for mountain scenery either among the Greeks, or the age of chivalry; or in the Renaissance, in a genuine way. Mountain scenery, wildness of impression, solitude, and loneliness, which is the pensive feeling of solitude: these are sources of great delight to vast numbers of men and women in our own time, and they were sources of unmitigated disgust to our great grand parents, or even a generation later. People looked on the mountain world as they did on the other world, with about as much idea of ever going to it of their own accord. Yet then, as now, and in all ages since Nimrod bent his first bow of primæval horn, or

Isaac went into the field to meditate, two, or let us say three, classes of men have belonged to the mountains, and the mountains to them. Monk, herdsmen, hunter ; prayer, food, pastime : these represent the three needs or crafts of men in a rough time, and their reign is in woods and hills, and all we call silvan and wild scenery. The sheep, and the goats, and the deer : to this day on the hills of Palestine you shall see the white sheep and black goats feeding together, one flock after another, and have one more gleam of light on the Lord's foreshadowing of Judgment. And to this day the deer and the sheep feed, avoiding each other, on highland moors; recalling, in the quaint symbolism of Nature, the ancient baptismal crosses and frescoes, where the sheep represent the Christian Church, and the hart thirsting for the waterbrooks is the heathen catechumen, desiring the waters of baptism.

Now, in my theory of landscape—highly incomplete as it is—I am only going to take into account the hunter and the monk, because they take to the hill voluntarily, as the modern painter does; they and their interests and thoughts are not confined to this or that valley, like the shepherd's ; in short, I speak of them as developed and educated persons— the one sadly taking his meditation, the other, if he be an

Englishman, mournfully taking his pleasure, amid mountain scenery. The only good St. Bernard could see in the mountains was that they are inhabited by the beasts; well, it is the nature of all Celts and Scandinavians, and most Teutons, to go to the mountains in search of the beasts. And modern mountaineering is only a variety of the chase, or takes the place of field sports: you get exercise — there is some risk to your neck, and your mind is fully and pleasantly employed without strain on it. No doubt a real painter will observe things very well, even though he likes woodcraft; and so far contemplation and sport may very possibly go together. But still we have the two sorts of men to this day, in modern phases: the hunter who goes to the hill for physical exercise, the monk who goes there for ascetic exercise. For I need hardly tell my audience that asceticism really means the taking of exercise, and that St. Paul's text, "Bodily exercise profiteth little," is not an encouragement to sedentary habits, but rather a caution against too great bodily austerities. Hunter and monk seek the hills even now; but there is another variety, the non-Christian recluse, who flees away, not to seek God, but avoid mankind: the Byronian or Shellevian, of whom the world is not worthy, or for whom it is perhaps too hot.

This sort of person will never make a painter, though he may write good enough verse. Read Lord Byron's description of the storm at Geneva, where—

> Jura bellows through her pitchy cloud
> Back to the joyous Alps, who call to her aloud.

Right good verse; but those who will read the passage will see that he cannot help comparing light and darkness to black eyes in women; in short, here, as elsewhere, all his view of Nature is passion-laden. He looks at the Alps in the dark mirror of his hatred of home—just as a French sketcher looks at them in his camera obscura. Both do good work, but neither can see good colour; and to this day Byron has, and deserves his determined admirers; and French landscape has, and deserves that amiable philosophe-persifleur, M. Taine, whom I do not in the least wish to disparage, for a great deal of what he says about English art is quite true — only there are principles of art anterior to the views of David and Ingres. And let us pass by the Byronian admiration of wild Nature or pure Nature, for it is only a form of the hatred of men. He is a monk, but too much in the way of his own Giaour, who makes such an unedifying end as a "lone Caloyer." The difference between him and the true, or "frömmer monch," is that he goes to the hills because he hates men; and the true monk because he hates the hills themselves. He care for their beauty, not he! He has given up his fellow-men, and embraced pain for its own sake; he will have no pleasure in snow, or pines, or gentianelle, or Alpine-rose. "We do not come here to look at the mountains," said the Carthusian of the Grande Chartreuse to him who asked wonderingly why the row of cells inhabited by the monks only looked into the dreary courtyard of the monastery, not on the valley of the Dead Guiers? This is the ancient knightly or mediæval view of the mountains as places of penance, marked far too contemptuously by Cervantes when he makes Don Quixote betake himself to nude penitential exercise in the Sierra. It is a genuine and formidable frame of mind: you have it in Launcelot as well as in Don Quixote. Don Quixote, as a character, is simply to be admired and imitated in every possible way, being a mirror of knighthood and gentlemanhood, and holding up to modern Englishmen the mirror of a great many qualities they ought to have, and sometimes have not. But this temper of mind is gone by from us; we must repent at home, and smart at home; and it is no more use to go into wild scenery to nurse one's spiritual wound, and grow better men, than it is to buy a stool to be melancholy upon, with a view to poetic composition. Retirement and meditation are good; but you can and must have them in a flat country also; we can't all have hermitages or live up trees; and those who desire to lead a life of repentance must do it where they stand.

At all events, the true Carthusian is no painter, nor will he make one. And yet the true painter will have something of the monk's spirit of loneliness in him. I cannot help thinking Mr. Ruskin's Carthusian must have been rather morose, or perhaps rather French; he may have embraced the opportunity of making a point; or of indirectly expressing his superiority to the Englishman's simple and sincere delight in earth, air, and water. But before I go to the truest and tenderest of Anglo-religious landscapists, whom I take to be Mr. Keble, there come two great names, who, in fact, are gigantic Caryatides at the gates of modern landscape art. They are Wordsworth and Scott; and nothing can more strongly confirm what has been said about the novelty of the British taste for landscape for its own sake in Wordsworth's time, than the hacknied saying that he created the taste by which alone he is to be enjoyed.

One cannot really put great geniuses into what

they call "a correct card;" and most well judging people must feel it very disagreeable when small men classify great ones. But there are beyond doubt two characters or sorts of men to whom the mountains are assigned, and who have in them the origin of the English love for scenery and mountain-drawing. It comes, I say, from the spirit of the hunter and of the monk. And I should say that Scott represents the former spirit in its highest form, and Wordsworth the other in its purest essence. One is active, the other contemplative. And here, like so many others, I must necessarily pay a tribute of general, particular, and unlimited respect to a man whose works I never delighted in as I ought to have done; though capable of feeling his greatness in many passages. Everybody must be able to see something like commanding grandeur in the character of the chief of two or three men who could live, poor, and beloved, and laborious, in this mercenary nineteenth century "on the hills like gods together, careless of mankind" as far as gain or getting on was concerned; but with power over and sympathy for all men together, and chiefly for simple life, for woodcutters and pedlars, and the afflictions of poor women. To read Wordsworth rightly one must simply ignore his defiant or self-confident passages, and that egotism which is unavoidable, when a man devouring his spirit alone, οἰοβώτας, speaks out his inner thoughts. Much of it came from early persecution and the fly-blowing of reviewers. It is his immense strength of humility with the humble and understanding of the simple; it is the deep all-searching heart, which makes Wordsworth so great; not the refinement or even the asceticism which he was proud of, but the sympathy which he had by the grace of God. Read him till you find enough to delight in; and get that by heart, or read it again and again, and every word of it will do you good. I suppose, with the mass of readers, his fame will always stand on the Indications of Immortality, and on the moral greatness which all men feel in him. I do not think a man who ate so many grouse as he must have eaten during his sojourn at the lakes, ought to have anathematized all field sports, as he seems to do in *Hartleap Well*. But his views as to the hunter place him for ever at the top of the contemplative class. Perhaps his crucial passage of description is that of the *Four Yews of Borrowdale*. And this I must say I have seen, that study of landscape and steady painting, and care for beauty of scenery, do much towards bringing the sporting painter ever nearer to the contemplative side, simply because he has not time for sport. But to say that the popular taste of English people for landscape is not closely connected with their love of chase and adventure; or to expect a man to care for a highland picture that does not remind him of grouse and deer; or to say he ought to like a representation of Swiss mountains that he don't want to get to the top of, that will not do either.* Nothing can be worse or more contemptible than what are called sporting pictures, as a rule, which dwell on the chase and the killing, not on the landscape. I need hardly mention them, I do not think of them; they are not art at all. Still the killing of game has to be done; those who object to it must not eat partridge or pheasant. And if the killing were wrong, it would demoralize men more than it does, so it seems to me, and make them unfit to enjoy and represent landscape, instead of filling them with delight in it. I cannot go into the subject: at all events you have Scott at the head of the active, and Wordsworth in command of the contemplative, brigade.

Now, this is why, to a landscape painter, Scott's

* I may say that Leech's caricatures escape condemnation, and rise to a very great height on the other side—partly from their perfection as character—partly from their admirable landscape. He never really knew his own great powers, I think. The Academy, as Mr. Millais implies in his evidence, ought to have taught him his own importance and rescued him from illustrating *Soapey Sponge*, &c. No man ever drew horse, dog, man or woman more brilliantly.

landscape stands before Wordsworth's — that he altogether forgets Scott in it. It is not greater, but simpler; and also there is more colour. Scott is of the old rejoicing, unanalytic race, who enjoyed scenery, they knew not why, and lost themselves in its simple and sincere pleasure. One cannot help feeling, even in the Indications of Immortality, the truth of the unusually wicked remark of our great critic, that Wordsworth cannot help congratulating Nature on having him to look at her. If so, as I have said, it is a consequence of the cheerful brutality of the critics of that remote period (of course there are no such people now) — in short, bullying only provokes self-assertion. Scott had no such trial: he was not compelled to self-analysis: people took what he wrote so easily and with such pleasure—in the *Border Minstrelsy* he hit at once on a national vein of feeling, and then he was essentially jolly, and could face the strongest toddy, when in search of original ballads. Morally, he had not indeed the hard training of the Englishman, the austere Dantesque honour, the content to live on little, desiring always less and less, without a thought of money-making or sale of his talents in the best market—all high thinking and low living. He who tempts by making rich, in some degree got the better of Scott. But before he thought of making a great fortune, and while he revelled in his vigour of life and strength, he *did* see with rapid bright intuition, and describe with fluent accuracy of observation, forgetting himself altogether in Nature. I said in the first lecture what a colourist he was. One cannot quote everything; but please look at the opening description of the *Lady of the Lake*, and the early part of the fifth canto; at the red sunset in *Rokeby*, at the description of Loch Coruishk in the *Lord of the Isles*, with the sail through the islands; and various descriptions in *Waverley*, *The Antiquary*, and *Guy Mannering*. In all these there is much Nature and little Scott: he is lost in delighted observation and record.

Wordsworth has to work out Wordsworth's thoughts of immortality on a May morning; he feels hardly up to it, he says, and has to invite a happy shepherd-boy to shout round him, and let him hear his shouts. Fancy the boy doing it now. Imagine him careering round the bard, as if round a snow-white ram determined to go the wrong way; waving his arms in the fervour of early droverhood. Imagine the "young varmint" shouting and tramping in lace-up highlows, and, finally, expecting sixpence. I can't get over it. I have enough boys of my own to know what they are like, and the noise they make is much more calculated to give me intimations of my mortality than of the contrary.

There is none of the Gothic laughter in Wordsworth: he is great, he is real, he is earnest, and all that, like life; but he does not, like life, admit the existence of cakes and ale; and they are real phenomena after all. And what you call the Gothic laughter is not exactly that of the buffoon or comic man. In its true form it justly points to blots and marks false notes, nor does it diminish, but enhance, the greatness of a great man. There must be men like Wordsworth or Dante—unaffectedly raised above others, not sharing the rudeness or the jollity of Homeric or Scandinavian gods and heroes. But we are ordinary beings, at least I am, very much so: I cannot breathe their empyrean very long, and I know it to be far above my own region. Scott was as true a Goth as Smid, the son of Troll—he is one of us: he puts Nature above himself. If you want to understand the Gothic laughter, read Scott on Davie Deans, and imagine the form of that elder in the action of " uttering his famous pamphlet called the *Cry of ane Howl in the Wilderness*." Contrast him with Duncan, of Knockdunder, and conceive that worthy's indignation,—" Pecause, when I talk to him of peasts, he answers me out of the Pible, which is not coot treatment for a shentlemans." Wordsworth's cataracts blow their trumpets from the steep to encourage him. Natural objects in Scott behave more naturally; he tells you what he saw or heard them do, and what he thought them like; so graphically in form, colour, and character, that he sets you beside them, forgetful of himself and yourself, and all but his scene; — coast, or lake, or hill-side, or sunset. And that is Art and Nature, or Naturalist Art. The other line is purist and philosophic, and perhaps a greater line, for him to whom it is given to follow it. But it will not make a sketcher, because you can't paint a waterfall blowing a trumpet.

Scott's greatness admits of the fellowship of smaller men, he having always lived contentedly with them, regarded by them for other reasons and qualities than those which made him great, and he suffered accordingly. Wordsworth's character and career were apart from all men, ascetic-contemplative: he could condescend to men of low estate, and love and understand the poor—that is to say, the Westmoreland peasantry, whom he knew. That is best of all; but he never met his equals, as equals, face to face. He went out from among us. And it is the worst sign about our modern society that earnest religion and high intellect alike seem to shrink from its venality or from its frivolity. Poets and parsons, if there be any sincerity or genuineness about them, care neither for political or local chicane, and therefore they are outcasts from the thoughts, the interests, and desires of nine-tenths of the male population of the realm. It is no use upholding spiritual motive before men whose motives are purely pecuniary: it is no use telling men that purely pecuniary motives will lead them to heaven, because they won't. That really seems to me one reason why the clergy are alienated, as the middle-class press is always saying, from the middle-class laity— because they cannot tell them how to serve God and mammon comfortably at the same time. And poets, like Wordsworth, earnestly desiring spiritual life, are, on the face of it, servants of anything but mammon, and just as entirely "alienated" from the lay Philistine as he is, who bids him give up dubious gain and gambling and meanness in the name of Christ.

It is with something like delight that I go on from Wordsworth—a great man of whom I really am not worthy, and Scott, as great, to me more loveable, but less pure and flawless in character—to a man who seems to me about the happiest of modern Englishmen in his life and death. I never saw Mr.

Keble but once; in Oxford of course; his name had been a household word for thirty years; yet in a place where public opinion goes by common-rooms and young men's sets, not by households at all; and where popularity generally lasts about six weeks, and seldom extends over two terms—he was reverently regarded by all who had regard for any spiritual thing. As his name is entirely identified with the Anglican Church, and as the Anglican Church is, for I do not know how many years to come, to be the subject of political agitation, his name will be defiled accordingly; he will be used and abused for party purposes. Yet by the grace given him, by favour of God in mind, education, and circumstance, he has done what nobody else has done so well; he has subjected a first-rate intellect entirely to the Faith; and served that first, and intellectual aspiration afterwards, with a pre-eminent singleness of choice. Being on a line of promotion, he deliberately let it pass him; having tangible power continually within reach, he said fair spiritual influence was enough for him; having command of the votes of many men, he chose rather to appeal to their souls. I have only to speak of his power of description in landscape: I wonder if it ever passed through his mind that he had any—probably not, or he never realized or cared for the fact. He seems to me an extraordinary man in modern times, because he was confessedly a genius without being a professional genius, devoted to the elaboration of himself in print; and a man of letters who put letters in their right and subordinate place in his own soul.

Here is a man, as far as I can speak of him without personal knowledge, who seems to have accepted success with a pre-eminent coolness and understanding, wonderfully unlike other men's. He seems to have taken impressions as they came, on a mind most sensitive, retentive and re-echoing, and to have uttered them again with wonderful simplicity, sometimes quietly, sometimes with conscious power, but always as the English parson, well informed in his form of the Faith, content to speak accordingly. But no one can doubt that Keble might have been a great popular describer if he had liked, who reads, "They know the Almighty's power," &c., or "Go up and watch the new-born rill;" or the many sketches of thorough English scenery and seasons, of willòws by the brooks, and their "lessons sweet of spring returning," and dun November days, and their red sunsets and golden leaves. These are incidentally given, for his mind, picturesque as it was, seems never to have turned aside to the picturesque in its pursuit of devout thought. And that is what men cannot understand. They can realize the fact that he did not care for promotion: they cannot imagine that he did not care for the praises of all reviews. The struggle for public success among intellectual and literary second-rates is so hard that they cannot understand a man ever undervaluing success who really can get it. "Artists are envious, and the world profane," said Heine,*: now here, in Keble the Anglican purist, you have a man in whom the Christian Faith has entirely cast out artistic envy. It is this recognition that great poetic success is not the chief good, to be sung, and scrambled, and toiled and intrigued for against rivals, which distinguishes him so much, and places him with Wordsworth and Scott, mighty ones who knew no envy. And I think the $\eta\theta$ος of the Church of England is manifested in this man's words, and also in his silence, in a manner worthy the attention of all who are capable of giving it. For that character is impressed with ancient English qualities, now attributed chiefly to the class called "gentle" men and women, but once honoured by all the race, before the days of self-advancement and equality and advertising. Nor have they died out

* "New Poems," by Prof. Arnold. "Heine's Grave."

of any class of us yet, I well trust. They are the qualities of reticence, of self-restraint, of love of barren honour, of preference of others' advantage to one's own; of practical sense of unworthiness, and acceptance of the rough side of things in faith. And these qualities make strong men and women; and the class which possesses them, as a class, will die very hard, and its strength will be best known, or only known, in its hour of danger.

This has nothing to do with landscape sketching, apparently, but in fact the connection is close. If you cannot submit to do without applause and success, you will not see genuineness of poetical character. If you do not care for genuineness of poetic character, you won't understand much about description. If you do not care for poetic description you will hardly see reality with anything of the painter's eye. And nothing, I think, encourages a painter so much as to find his own observations confirmed in poetry, and to see what he has recorded in form and colour "done" also in cunning words. Therefore read as much Wordsworth and Scott as ever you can; I take it for granted that everybody who cares for landscape at all has Tennyson pretty well by heart. I am not going to talk about the Laureate, because he has been reviewed, analyzed and adored;

lectured upon and concordanced, and sat upon, and sat at the feet of, and had meanings discerned in him, and been intellectually manipulated over to that extent that one's thoughts about him seem reduced to the consistency of mashed potatoes; pleasing but inorganic.

But get all you can of him by heart, and you will be glad of it afterwards; especially the early poems: their landscape and music together will be no small help to your landscape and colour: he requires a course of lectures with illustrations. And if you will only get enough line-drawing into your work, and get forms right, I do not see why you should be denied considerable license in the use of your imagination or fancy. If you can really draw, try and illustrate Tennyson if you like; or take subjects from the endless gallery of that true painter-poet, the author of *Jason* and the *Earthly Paradise*. If you can't help imagining what a scene, or a place, or an event really looked like at such a time, and a notion of what it was like comes to you, and you want to draw it, do draw it, only draw it right at your peril. You should not of course think of drawing landscape you have not seen; that can lead to nothing but childish failure; but a certain license of composition you ought to have. You would not like to write poetic descriptions in bad grammar : you would like to cut your verses or your sentences to a point always, like pencils ; and in the same way you ought not to be able to bear pictures or sketches in which good feeling strives with bad drawing. And cling to Turner and out-door subjects, or natural still-life, like shells and flowers, as soon as you are fit to practise them ; that is to say, as soon as you can draw well in free-hand and from models.

LECTURE IX.

ART, CRAFT, AND SCHOOLS.

IN my last practical lecture, it may, perhaps, be thought a doubtfully good recommendation to young students to begin from Nature and with the brush, as soon as they have learnt a little what correct outline and fine gradation are, by practice with the chalk or soft-point. Now, in the first place observe, I partly said then, and I now say, that you must faithfully use pen and sepia in all your work, as in copies from Holbein and the *Liber Studiorum*. And further, I am sure that study from these masters and from Nature will, from the first and throughout, make up to you whatever deficiencies may exist in the course of our Art-schools. It must be remembered that in their origin they were hardly meant to be artistic at all; only meant as schools where artizans could learn to draw patterns, and if possible, to invent them. Then people found, under Prof. Ruskin and others, that to invent means a great deal, that you can't get good Art out of nothing, or have good patterns without good Art; that is to say, without the study of the highest forms of painting and sculpture: since all excellent ornament and decoration was derived from schools of drawing and sculpture of the great human subject. So the Art-schools must now afford instruction in the highest forms of Art. You cannot teach men to invent ornament, if they only study ornament: that is to say, other men's inventions. You cannot do a good design of your own without study of your own from Nature; with it, you may do anything, according to your capacity, and you may progressively enlarge your capacity. There may be mechanical work, and hands without brains; and I consider it an evil. But looking at our Art-schools only in the commercial point of view, they were intended to enable our decorative manufacturers to learn to design patterns of their own, not merely to copy other people's. Therefore your schools must aim at producing painters. The success of Mr. Burchett at the Royal Academy is now yearly emulated by many of his pupils, I trust. But I think the prize system as well as the training course now requires modification in some such way as the following.

Much has been said, not only brilliantly but rightly, on the need of clear thought in this country, as opposed to the spirit of mere labour. It is a deficiency, the deficiency in all our people, that they think, imagine, invent too little, and work too hard. To be hard at work anyhow is enough, because it puts away the malady of thought—few people seem to look on thought as a valuable thing meant to lead them right. If a man be fully employed, that is considered enough for him, whether he be employed in a degrading and mindless way, or in noble and developing labour. This is the principle on which our great industrial fortunes are made. Huge profits are obtained by division of labour; the operations of work are subdivided till the most of the workers acquire only a monotonous and contemptible dexterity; and men get mindless in making pin-heads, or turning screws and washers. I believe that work was meant to be enjoyed as well as endured. It is a part of the curse that is on the earth; but those who endure it patiently and well generally find it easier. Artistic feeling is an alleviation of toil. And so men whose work has no pleasure or thought in it are naturally malcontents in all trades; they get thinking, as they say, and that is an evil instead of a good. And they are not altogether wrong, for they suffer by limitation of their intelligence through over-division of labour ; it takes from them the mental development they ought to gain from their work. But I have observed also, even in the higher handicrafts, (as with carpenters and masons, for example) that men's minds get sadly limited, so as to care only for what they can do well themselves, and that they learn not only indifference, but contempt for higher things. If a man can make a box or chest he takes his stand on its utility, and does not see that it would be any better for being carved, or he any better for carving it ever so well. In short, our English motto, "Do one thing well," will not bear pressing too far ; and the mass of English people always do press every notion too far. It seems as difficult for a man to get hold on an idea as it is for him to get a horse to suit him ; but he will infallibly ride either to death when he has got it, and never have another if he can help it. And so in the lower walks of life one or two operations seem to be enough for a mind. That is why we can't get Art or good patterns out of the English artizans ; because they are not artizans, and never learn a whole Art, or to do anything they can take pride or pleasure in. They are not taught any Art properly by the capitalist, who is the master-tradesman ;—whereas all high or liberal Art must be taught by the master's hand. Now the Art and Science schools and examinations are at length established by the State: to do the work, and give the education which the capitalist ought to have provided. And I am naturally anxious that the teaching which they afford should come into proper workable contact with other education, with that of the primary schools if possible; and I desire greatly to see the best boys in parish schools have opportunities and proper training for the art-and-science examinations. The schools are there, and all kinds of young people connected with trade and commerce, and sometimes real working men, come into them.

And here I must quote a few lines from Professor Huxley: I had not seen them when I wrote what has just gone before, and I need not say with what satisfaction I came upon them in his *Lay Sermons and Lectures*, p. 62:—" A great step in this direction (that of general scientific education) has already been made by the establishment of science-classes under the Department of Science and Art—a measure which came into existence unnoticed, but which will, I believe, turn out to be of more importance to the welfare of the people than many political changes, over which the noise of battle has rent the air. Under these regulations, a schoolmaster can set up a class in one or more branches of science : his pupils will be examined, and the State will pay him at a certain rate for all who succeed in passing." Last year the Professor had about 2,000 sets of papers, and the mathematical examiners twice as many.

But State Art-teaching has to be more or less adapted to the pupils; that is to say, to what they can do, and what they like to do. For it is quite impossible to prevent the wishes and ideas of the whole body of pupils in a school from bearing on what is taught, or anyhow on what is learnt. Consequently teaching is somewhat narrow and mechanical; and it limits itself too often to dexterity in the operations of Art, mere learning the use of the tools, without remembering that the tools are to be used really to interpret Nature and express thought. So that the competitive system, and the way in which prizes are allotted, seems now to require modification; as ministering to this English admiration for labour as against thought, and the English taste for mere dexterity in minor operations, which excludes advance, and progress, and honourable effort at something worthy of beings with minds. People cannot see that, though it is indispensable to learn to copy a cast rightly, it is not much to have done it ; but that learning to do it is only a lesson towards learning to do something from Nature rightly, and invent something again from that, and go on from that, sailing for evermore on the Sempre-si-fa-maggiore. He who can do one thing well is persuaded there is nothing else worth doing. We want men and women in every class of life to possess and develop some of the artistic faculties; some of that power of mental vision which sees character and seizes on marked features; and to have some hand education, sufficient for ability to record it. We want more thought, quicker insight, more pleasure in gaining hold on new truth. For knowledge is gain, and fresh truth is fresh life, in the most literal sense, to any who has learned to care for the culture of his own spirit. And the ordinary education or non-education of poor men in England is all against this; on one hand, they are told they must be content with their station, and must never think about anything except what they are taught by the S. P. C. K.; on the other, if they are town workmen, they are spoken of and treated as mere hands; they are not taught to take pleasure in invention or progress; if they have any thought, it is to get more money for less work. The feeling of a good workman, who does his very best with time and material for the work's sake, is strictly artistic. Though he may not work at fine Art but at rough, the true craftsman is the artist at heart: or he would be, were it not for his indifference to progress and the narrowness of his interest in his craft. High and low, they are all the same: an engraver has learnt to imitate mist effect very nicely, and that is all he cares for in his work, and he tells you that Albert Dürer did not know much about aërial perspective. Exactly in the same way a carpenter who can take off shavings exquisitely well does not think of drawing or carving, but remains content with a quasi-artistic manipulation of shavings. Exactly in the same way do some excellent artist-masons, great friends of mine, having learnt to cut several varieties of lily rather well, go on carving lilies till I am sick of the sight of them, and, in fact, till the mechanical unenjoyed work is sickening. Now you'll excuse my saying that the present Art-teaching and competition system ministers to this.*

* The usual training by straight lines, and drawing curves by the use of such lines, seems occasionally to make the pupil ignore curve altogether, and literally finish his work on the forms of its straight blocking-out. There are leaves, nicely arranged and cut leaf patterns, on capitals and spurs of the pillars of the Oxford Museum, where all the leaf curves are utterly lost, character entirely missed, and the sides of them mere straight lines, bent or cut to awkward points, with great central ribs. Our pupils must not rest in knowing how to draw straight lines in order to imitate curves; they must know that Nature is all curves, and pursue the beautiful ones with choice and feeling.

It is monotonous; it leads only to knowledge of the use of tools, and allows people to go on too long in mere competitive dexterity.

Grown persons go on for ever doing light-and-shade copies of casts. At present I believe the principle is that a student of any age, who has not got a prize, may go in for any of the prizes; but that, having once obtained a prize, he cannot have it again, or any inferior one. This I have no doubt did capitally when there were but few pupils fit to compete at all; but now great general attention has been drawn to the prizes: there is a crowd competing for them, as there should be; but very few of all that crowd have an idea beyond getting a medal for dexterity in stippling and hatching. They get to think there is nothing to look for in Nature but objects to stipple and hatch, and no reward except medals. Competition is good for school-teaching perhaps, but it is very bad for the competing artist; it shuts his eyes to everything which does not pay. Besides, harmless pleasure in mere neat execution grows to vanity; one gets a bronze medal; and straightway all the energies of one's being are concentrated on getting a gold one. I don't know what becomes of the gold medallists; I hope they turn out painters; but I should think a good many of them were in danger of becoming mercenary, and thinking only of selling pictures, not of painting them ; or of growing conceited and priggish, and so falling into the hopeless region of the third-rate.

Another thing has struck me in looking over exhibitions of prize drawings under the department system, and that is that hard-point drawing, the use of pen and ink or sepia, or of the point of the brush as a drawing instrument, is hardly enough encouraged. I certainly should like to see some prizes for etching on copper, by advanced students ; or for good studies from Rafael's or Michael Angelo's fine-lined drawings with hard pencil on metal point. The more skilful draughtsmanship we can get from our engravers the better. The fact is a great deal has been taught and learnt in these schools since they began, and I should say the standard of their competition work ought to be advanced,—perhaps somehow in this way. I would have a stringent superannuation law as to all the lower Department prizes for the object or mere still life. After such an age or after so many years of competition, in either or both, the student shall compete no more in that class or for that prize. It will not do to have a number of senior pupils, especially ladies with great command of leisure, competing year after year in copying casts, and hatching and stippling their lives away, under the impression that they are studying art, whereas they are only sticking, not very fairly, in the way of younger students. I should like to see a senior department of competition, where the prizes should be all for work from Nature. They would have to be carefully classified, of course; and might be broadly divided into works in light and shade, and works in colour: the prizes should be very varied, ranging from oil landscape or figures, painted up for exhibition, down to three-hour sketches in the open air, and studies of single objects, as a stone or a branch with a few leaves. I include also decorative treatment and analysis of flowers, &c. After three or four times, or a term of years' competing, in the cast or object school, I should superannuate a student whether he or she has gained a prize or not, and I should send him into the Nature-competition school. If a medallist, or at least a prizeman, he might go in without examination. If not so distinguished, I should make him do a simple drawing in a given time in school, to be sure he had skill enough to be allowed to compete. Then the subjects should be gradated in difficulty, and nobody should compete more than a stated number of times; and I think I would settle that sending in a very bad drawing should exclude the unfit competitors for the next year, always getting rid of the worst by a preliminary trial also, as in the Middle class Examinations. You see there is no pity in competition, if we are to have it. A drawing is either good enough, in promise or performance, or it is altogether too bad. The difficulty of every school and system of instruction is to know what to do with the fourth-rates, with those who cannot have anything but their labour for their pains. I hold that that is enough; I think every one who tries honestly to get artistic skill will succeed in finding happy employment; but he ought not to run against others if he cannot win. Competition interferes with true feeling; it takes away singleness of mind, and care for art and Nature only. I have said it reduces art to medal-hunting in the first place, and picture dealing in the second. At present I suppose it must continue, but I dislike it altogether, and should be glad to think that art-students in England had a little more in them of the fire that is not the fire of gain or of contention. "They that run in a race run all." It is curious how St. Paul appeals to the full energies of his hearers by the image of a race, rejecting at the same time the idea of competition one against the other, and bidding all so run that they may obtain. The spiritual life of faith and the spiritual life of art are led on the same conditions of hope in the unseen.

And this brings us back to what we started with, that art is a spiritual object in itself, not a mere pursuit of fame or money. "This does not come with houses or with gold." We believe it to be capable of developing and elevating the spirit of man; as an energy or pursuit, irrespectively of what is popularly called success. And it is impossible, as we said, to agree as to what success is : to one man it is to do, or know, good things ; to another to get nice things ; to a third, to be thought that which he is not. These lectures concern the first of these classes only ; and we began them by setting forth what the study of naturalist art might do in a humble way for ordinary people—saying that what we desired most was art for the people, and that, if any great stride in advance is made in our time, it will be probably made by some man from among the multitude, like Blake or Turner ; and that popular art-education on any sound principles must always give greater chances of awakening genius and drawing out power from thence. And I speculated on a systematic connexion and working together, one day, of our Science and Art Department with primary and secondary schools ; in the hope of organizing public examination and competitive education, so as, as far as possible, to neutralize the bad moral effect of that continued intellectual money scramble, to which it seems our generation is doomed. For as yet there is no sign that any great class of English people care for learning or thought, or the work of intellect, or anything that does not pay in money. And as you cannot keep up an art-school without medals, so your only chance of pressing on education anywhere is to tell the rich they can't keep their dominant position without it, and the poor that they cannot live without it at all. Of course there are endless exceptions and admixtures of higher character: the spread of popular education will really be brought about by the good qualities of the British people, and not by their bad ones—by their general benevolence, not by their great covetousness. You *may* get a town full of rough people to grow less rough; but only by individual appeal to the goodwill and benevolence which is in them, and which you can only develop by showing goodwill of your own to them. And the great lesson and confession of the Education Bill is that this is done in this country mainly on Christian principles and by Christian people, and that it cannot be done without Christianity: culture won't work without love; and when you deal with that you deal with Him who is Love, and He with you.

Then we said something of the need of culture

in England, and of natural beauty and its study as a means of culture, and how the hideous life we lead by making this country the workshop of the world, and ourselves, consequently, the spinners and stokers of creation, shuts off natural beauty altogether from many who might be happy in it. I did not express any hope about our one day leaving off spinning a little, and not stoking quite so hard, or our ceasing to infect our own air and poison our own rivers; I should be very glad to do so if I could. And we said that art was a spiritual thing; and art-work an expression of the delight of man's spirit in the beauty of God's work. We also took note of a passage in Exodus, and others in the New Testament, which speak of diversities of gifts, and of the artistic gift as a gift of the Spirit of God. We divided art thus. It might be expression of (delight in) ideal or spiritual beauty, saying that in the highest forms of beauty in Divine perfection, the ideal and spiritual coincided. Also, we said art-work might be applied to man's uses, especially to education, which is spiritual, and to enjoyment of common life and commerce, which is tangible; and we saw that art is not really applied to use till good works of common art and common life are brought within the reach of the people. And I did not say then what I say now, that I cannot see why a carpenter should not learn drawing enough to enable him to carve, or a mason either. The Ammergau work, in particular, shows what may be done, and it would fill up times of bad weather and health, or of slack work. Nor did I say (what I think Yorkshire and possibly Norfolk men may know better than I do), what capital surface-carved oak used to be in the cottages and farms all over the West Riding, done for love and for pleasure; as genuine art-work in a humble way as Rafael's frescoes are in a grand way. Then, having settled that art as the interpreter of God's work in Nature was a good thing, we considered that it is an old thing, and that such as we have is connected with such as the Greek race had in early days; and we began to consider some of the qualities which enabled them to take such a lead, and position of command, in symbol-interpretation of Nature. We find that, after their lights, they, that is to say, their greatest "exemplaria," did what we wish to do in our best moments, and made their art a liturgy or ministry or service to their gods. We saw that the Greek in search of God traced Him by certain foot and hand-marks in Nature without, and in his own spirit and moral life within: that, like other nations, he thought that somebody made the rain and fruitful seasons and their beauty, and that somebody also made right and right-dealing persons; and from his notions of beautiful and right-doing men he got various wonderful conceptions of what the upper powers of right and Nature must be like. The best men, we said, would get farthest in this search, feeling after one God, each according to his light. Then we said, symbolic Nature-worship became idolatry, because Greeks insisted on seeing or being shown God in their own form, and lost hold of righteousness and of Him, and so lost unity, and disregarded household love and honour of women; and that as they lost hold on right, and lost hope of finding the Doer of right, their art fell all into technical dexterity or sensual trifling; and their idolatry became first earthly, then sensual; then at length devilish, when the faith arose and defied the false gods. Accordingly, we saw that Christianity could not be expected to pay much attention to statues of Apollo and Athene, because Christians had been so often burnt and tortured in the name of Apollo and Athene. But as to the use of art for teaching any good thing, or giving any harmless pleasure to men, it seemed that Christians of the second century were quite as willing to use it as we are now; and that such art as was possible, in the sudden blackness of darkness which began with Alaric, was continued by religious men for religious purposes, there being no possibility of any one else's doing so, between York and Constantinople. That is, A.D. 410, marks the end of Græco-Roman Art; and nothing but Byzantinism remains until the earliest Lombard work about Verona and Pavia in the eleventh century. Rome, and especially Ravenna, are the cities where the great mosaics still remain to show the extraordinary gift of colour which was still left, or rather which seems to have sprung up between Greek and Ostrogoth. Placidia, Theodoric, and Justinian are the three names with whom these works are connected, and those three names span the extreme darkness of Italy from desolation to desolation, from Attila to Alboin. That is to say, Galla Placidia died in the same year when Attila was beaten back on Northern Italy, from Chalons, in 450—centre of fifth century. And Narses invited Alboin at the end of Justinian's reign in 568. . . . Torcello was then built, the mother city of Venice. With Alboin and the Lombards, hammer-men all, begins the Lombard sculpture of Verona, with its realism of huntings and battles, its historical record of Scripture and the faith, and its griffin symbolism, which repeated, strangely, and for the last time in sincere purpose, the Mosaic and divinely-prescribed symbol of the Cherub. That is all till the eleventh century, when a new architecture begins the great Renaissance of art at Pisa, under Lombard and Byzantine forms of extreme beauty, when the Pisan Duomo and Baptistery and the leaning Campanile were built, to contend with the piazzas of Florence and Venice (and I think successfully) for the title of the most perfect group of buildings of any age or time. That is at the end of the eleventh century. Nicolas of Pisa marks the early thirteenth century; Cimabue and Giotto the late thirteenth century. There is a century of Giotteschi; Masaccio, and a constellation arise in the fifteenth century; and at its end Ghirlandajo is dying, and Michael Angelo is rising in Florence and Rafael in Urbino. John Bellini was near his end in Venice, when Dürer was there in 1506 : Holbein had been born in 1498. Design and drawing are perfected by these men ; and in the next century (sixteenth) colour is perfected in the Venetian school, which centres in Titian, Tintoret, and Veronese : just after whose time Velasquez is in Spain and Italy, the aloe-flower of Spanish art.

After Veronese art has finally given up the service of religion and betakes herself to mythology, completing the change which Rafael began. The best men left go with Nicolo Poussin and Claude to portrait and landscape and pastoralism. And the Dutch and Flemish school rises in beautiless strength, with Rembrandt, Rubens, and Cuyp at its head; Rubens being big enough for equal division between mythology, portrait, and landscape. There is nothing new till Hogarth, Gainsborough, Blake, and Turner, whose lives overlap. There is a skeleton of the historical part of these lectures to help your memory.* Take the three epochs, Greek and Græco-Roman, Byzantine, Florentine : and the leading names and times thus in a mnemonic. I always prefer to remember history by groups of names and events, men and their deeds, to getting it up by dates.

V. century B.C. Marathon—Phidias—Elgin Marbles.
V. century A.D. Alaric—Theodoric—Ravenna.
        Giotto to Angelo, XIV.—XVI.

Remember that Phidias was done to death in 432, outbreak-year of Peloponesian war; that Mummius took Corinth, B.C. 146; that Græco-Roman art came to an end in Alaric's great year, 410; that Ghirlandajo was four years old when Muhammad II. took Constantinople in 1453; that Lorenzo de Medici died in Columbus' year (1492); that Albert

* See Memorial Chart.

Dürer's great work was published in the Flodden year (1513); that Veronese died in the Armada year (1588); that Turner ceased to exhibit (dying two years after) in the Exhibition year, 1851.

I do not lay much stress on the usual employment of the word Renaissance, as it applies to art. There is no doubt about the revival of letters in the fifteenth and sixteenth centuries; but art, which teaches without letters, had begun to revive when the Lombard chisels began to work in St. Zenone and St. Ambrogio, at Milan, at Pavia, and at Lucca. Also, I am inclined to protest against your thinking of Florentine sculpture as derivative, and based on imitation of Greek models. Nicolo Pisano and others were helped by Greek models; but their energies and their objects were alike their own. No broken-nosed antiques were needed to teach the blood of Alboin and Agilulf that beauty is beautiful; and as they never reached the Greek perfection in representing the body and limbs, so no Greek ever approached, or thought of, or sought for, their power of facial expression.

Then we had a lecture on Symbolism: from the Cherub and Griffin, through the Catacombs and the Ravennese mosaics; through the history of the Cross and the Crucifix; and the parallel systems of illuminating churches with fresco for poor men who could not read; and illuminating missals and Evangeliaries for rich people, who read more pleasantly and intelligently with the pictures. Also, we said that the mysteries of the Middle Ages appeared to have been intended for sound doctrinal instruction, however abused they probably may have been; and we referred to the last surviving example of them— the Passions-Vorstellung of Ober-Ammergau in Bavaria. And I maintained that there is a symbolic tradition, so to speak, running through all Christian times, from the earliest to the latest; that it is used continually to enforce and impress the truth of the Lord's Incarnation and Death for Man; and to teach how that was foretold or foreshadowed in the history of Israel, in the Law and the Prophets, by sacrifice and other typical actions, and also by typical persons. In fact, that there has been a system of Church-symbolism, or preaching in picture; and that the ancient subjects of decoration in Catholic Churches, besides representations of the Person and Humanity of the Saviour, are, properly speaking, the typical persons, objects and events of the Old Testament, and the Miracles of Mercy in the New.

We also made some remarks on the serious and comic grotesque, illustrating what was said by examples from Albert Dürer, Hans Holbein, and Michael Angelo; and occupied two lectures with comparison or contrast between Dürer and Holbein, Rafael and Buonarotti. Then we betook ourselves to practical considerations on landscape drawing from Nature, examining the meanings of various terms and rules. It appeared that drawing in the open air is like drawing anywhere else, only more difficult: first, for want of comforts and appliances; secondly, for want of time, since Nature is always changing, and no scene is the same for any length of time together. Success then depended, as it seemed, first in possessing, or becoming possessed with, a definite leading idea, or feeling, in our work, and understanding how to make the feature of the picture which conveys our leading idea the principal feature to all spectators. Thus, in a lake scene, whose leading idea is calm, we shall probably call attention to the reflections in its calm depths, or the solid motionless forms of rocks in repose. In a torrent sketch, where force and violence of motion is our leading idea, the lines of broken hurrying water, and wreaths of falling or flying foam, will probably have to be made chief features by being placed in the principal light, or they may be made prominent by other means. By examining some of Turner's etchings of the principal lines of his subjects we saw, that artful arrangements of line, and still more of light and shade, have much to do with leading the eye of the spectator to the artist's chosen points in the picture, and that the whole science of composition consisted in this—to have a leading thought to express, to get it into the principal place in your picture, and to surround it with accessory or minor facts bearing upon it, and explaining or enforcing it : causing the eye by their arrangement to enter the picture as if it were a real scene, and to understand the proper bearings and relations to each other of all the facts in it. Turner's power of leading the eye an unconscious captive, by force of drawing and artful use of perspective, were just glanced at ; also the extraordinary significance and expressive power of his line-drawing. It seemed that such clinging to the leading idea would give that greatly-desired quality called character to our work, because the leading idea of everything is in its *character* or principal *marking;* also that the universally-applicable precept of Mulready, to know what one has to do and do it, was no other, in fact, than an exhortation to choose the main and vital feature to draw on one's paper, and draw it with proper adjuncts in proper places. Easy to say and hard to do, no doubt; but the methodical effort to seize on main features becomes easier with practice; and also the tenacity of the mind in holding by a leading feature, through all the changes and chances of various operations of realization may be greatly increased by practice also. And on clearness and tenacity of view depends our knowledge what we are really going to do, and how to do it.

My last lecture was a scrambling Theory of English Naturalist Landscape, based on rough analysis of the English love of Nature, especially of wild scenery; and illustrated by reference to three great names in poetry, Scott, Wordsworth, and Keble. I omitted Tennyson, because his descriptions range over the whole school of English landscape, that is to say, all representation of every phase of scenery; and would require a long course of lectures, illustrated from Turner and others. It would be well, indeed, if somebody would write them; but he must be a strong landscape painter and observer, whenever he arises. Some of us probably know the difficulty of finding a good poetical description of high Alpine scenery. They will perhaps remember how painfully so excellent a describer as Rogers fails, in the short poem called *Morning on the Alps*, purely from never having seen what he is describing; how he talks of chasing roebuck (he means chamois) through the snow with hound and horn (you might as well pursue salmon with hound and horn); how he seems to imagine that an alpenstock is made of iron, and used as a leaping-pole for giant bounds from one aiguille to another. That is failure, by a man who did not often fail. For partial success, there are some good lines of glacier description in Kingsley's *Saint's Tragedy;* and Coleridge's well-known *Hymn in the Valley of Chamounix,* is good, though rather general in its description. We all know the difficulty; and let those who want to see it overcome, and to see the whole spirit of high landscape in a small octavo page and a half, read the Idyll at the end of the Princess, "Come down, O Maid." The Slade Professor at Oxford once pronounced it to me "the finest piece of pure description in English or any other language," and I think he was simply right. There is no time to read it now, and most of us would like to take time over it.

Well, last lecture came to this: that English people generally liked Alpine scenery for the sake of adventure, and the excitement of wild natural form; or else because they enjoy the sensation or emotion of loneliness. And we said, when you can draw rightly you are right in indulging your imagination, and drawing subjects illustrative of other men's thoughts; but that, bright as your imaginations may be, nothing will make up for your pictures being ill drawn, false or forced in light and shade, or muddy in colour. A good idea in bad perspective is thoroughly disgusting; and particularly so if it is a borrowed idea, and you are setting a poet's description all wrong in another person's eye. Just as a bad description of his work to a painter, is a bad illustration of his work to a poet. It is an injustice; it spoils his idea by misinterpretation; and all incompetent or superfluous criticism is of the same nature.

And once more, in conclusion, let me just say how important it seems to me that everybody should learn some kind of art or craft. Women are better off than men very commonly, in as far as they can all make something. Stockings, or shirts, or puddings are really good things; and it is certainly better to be able to make, than only to eat and wear out. We are always reading of highly-educated men who have to act as sheep-washers or shoe-blacks, or unskilled labourers in the colonies, because they can't make a nail on the anvil, or solder the bottom of a kettle, or dovetail the sides of a box together, or shoe a horse, or rub him down, or know how many feeds a day he ought to have in work; or make a pea-jacket, or even sew on a button, or milk a cow, or know how long it takes to roast a leg of mutton, or whether, if you want to boil it, you should put it in hot water or cold to begin with. The traditionary school-games, I know, give strength, activity, and harmonious action of hand and eye. It is a question, however, whether some time might not be taken from games, and given to any art or craft a lad may fancy. Drawing and music, I have no doubt, flourish here, and perhaps at present one can hardly ask for more. But all lads like carpentering, and in my time I had enough of the Northman in me to become a bit of a smith. I should think that all schools ought to compete for Whitworth's craftsman-scholarships, if it were only to learn what a craft is worth. It is a thing I should desire for myself and my sons to understand a craft or minor art as well as a fine art, or a working man's work as well as my own. As I would desire that a smith should know something of drawing for refinement, so I think a gentleman should be able to make a nail, for understanding of hand-craft. And also, that he and the craftsman may understand each other. For as I said before, the craftsman's view is but narrow : and he cannot believe that any gentleman has cunning of hand enough to know the value of skilled labour. Nor does he understand the connexion between Culture and Design. I remember somebody in the glass business once set up his throat against the late Lord Derby because he had translated Homer and couldn't make a glass. If he himself had been able to make a glass fit to be seen there would have been more in his observation; but as a British glassmaker he probably could do nothing except what was rather ugly and expensive.

Just before this lecture was first delivered I had the dissatisfaction of comparing a Venice glass, blown at once with little time or labour, graceful, serviceable, lovely in wandering veins of transparent colour, with an English chimney ornament, useless, laborious, painted here, engraved there, cut in this place, crosscut in that, utterly dull and tasteless in shape and decoration, and costing probably about four times the price of the Venetian. Classical knowledge would teach our glass-workmen better forms if they had it. But every man should know a craft, that is quite true, especially all whom the craftsman calls "swells." You know so much more of the great mass of men when you know something of their work: you are so much more at one with them when they know you appreciate their skill and the worth of their hands' cunning: it is a mutual understanding. "I must have you gentlemen to pull and draw with the men," said Francis Drake ; and he got a very considerable place in history on that principle. Read the passage about Amyas Leigh and the Elizabethan discipline at sea, when all adventurous Englishmen were one, gentle and simple, friends bound in ties of strictest discipline—soldiers, sailors, craftsmen, hunters, terrible and beloved by land and sea. And that discipline was inherited from the noble training of early feudal times, which was quite as democratic, between gentle blood and gentle blood, as it was strict in gradation of rank below the salt. A good knight was the equal of kings, and might have kings' sons among his pages to clean his spurs and hold his stirrup. Something like this exists still with squires of the right sort, and their out-of-door servants. And I trust it is so, in many trades, between masters and workmen ; but all division of labour, all mindless work and complication of mechanism, goes sadly against it. To ride and shoot thoroughly well are the craft of the hunter ; and woodcraft is equal in value as a possession of the body and mind to knowledge of any other craft ; but in this country it comes in only as an expensive amusement. I am not going to say anything against cricket or the traditionary games, though I used always to like rowing best. Football has a symbolic value, I suppose, because it teaches one to shin and cut down one's fellow-creatures all through life. Still I think learning a craft worth something to every boy.

And here we come to the end of a lecture and the beginning of a subject. These papers may end here. The connexion between Art and Poetry, archæology and history, is daily better understood, and they may, I trust, be a contribution in that direction. It matters little if they close arbitrarily, for there is no end to talk of art, and the skill that wins grace. As Aristotle said, "The end is in the energy,"—and the labour is the reward. As Tennyson says,—

> We know the merry world is round
> And we may sail for evermore.

—sail away at last into the sunrise, like Turner's Ulysses—so may it be with all of us.

THE END.

London: Printed by SMITH, ELDER AND Co., Old Bailey, E. C.

MEMORIAL CHART.

I divide Art, or accessible Works of Art, before the Cinquecento, into two epochs of about 1,000 years each.

1. Greek or Græco-Roman (say 500 B.C.), from Ageladas and Phidias to taking of Rome by Alaric, 410 A.D.; taking 125 B.C. (capture of Corinth by Mummius) as transition date from Greek to Græco-Roman.

2. Byzantinism and the successive artistic Renaissances, Ostrogothic (?) Lombard, Pisan, Florentine; till Italo-Gothic skill in Drawing culminates in Rafael and Michel Angelo. Let this begin with the Ravennese work of Fifth Century, and end with 1492 (Columbus' year, and death of Lorenzo de Medici), six years before the birth of Holbein; Michel Angelo, seventeen years old; Rafael, nine.

Epoch I.—Greek and Græco-Roman, Sixth Century B.C. to Fifth Century A.D.
Culminating Period, that of Athenian Supremacy, from Persian to end of Peloponnesian War, 490-405.

First School. Traces of Spiritual Motive. Fifth and Sixth Centuries B.C.	*Second School.* Naturalism verging on Sensualism. Fourth and Third Centuries B.C.	*Third School.* Græco-Roman (including Rhodian Work), or *Academic School* of Science and Eclectic Copying
Masters. { Ageladas.		
{ Phidias. Myron. Polycletus.	Praxiteles. Scopas. Lysippus.	Cleomenes. Agasander. Athenodorus, &c.
Accessible Works. { Elgin Marbles. Two Discoboli (copies), &c.	Faunus, Aphrodites (copies), &c.	Laocoon, &c., considered as a work of Pliny's age. Nude Germanicus (?).

[Græco-Roman Art may be said to end where Byzantinism has its origin, i.e., in the Early Christian sepulchral work in fresco, mosaic, and bas-relief, from Second Century to Fifth Century.]

Epoch II.—Byzantinism to Early School of Florence, and so on to Cinquecento (450 (say) to 1492 A.D.)

GREEK WORKS in Foreign Cities (al. or Cities of Refuge (?).	LOMBARD CHURCHES, (*e.g.*):—	FLORENTINE SCHOOL of Drawing, Eleventh Century to Cinquecento.
(a) Ravenna, 450-568.	(a) { St. Ambrogio, Milan. St. Michele, Pavia. Duomo, Lucca. } Seventh Century.	Cimabue. Giotto (Giottesi?), died 1336.
[Attila to Alboin, Chalons to Forum Julii.] Placidia. Theodoric. Justinian.	{ St. Zenone, Verona. } Eleventh Century.	Orgagna, died in 1376. Van Eyck, 1366. Angelico, died 1455. Pupil, Benozzo Gozzoli. Masaccio, died 1429.
(b) Torcello, Duomo of. Sixth to Eleventh Centuries.	(b) Pisan or Lombard-Byzantine. Bonaventura, Tenth and Eleventh Centuries. Niccolo Pisano, Twelfth Century.	Ghirlandajo, died 1495. At Bologna, Francia, born 1450.
Venice: St. Mark's.		Michel Angelo, born 1475. Correggio, born 1494. Rafael, 1483, at Urbino: with Perugino and Pinturicchio.

Cinquecento: Venetian School of Colour, &c. Moderns.

Remember these years:—1504. Year of Rafael's Sposalizio and Michel Angelo's Cartoon of Pisa; Leonardo at Florence (Standard), Luini his great Lombard pupil, Holbein his disciple. 1506. Dürer at Venice, with John Bellini and Carpaccio, both near their end: Giorgione and Titian in 1510: Luther, Rafael, and Michel Angelo in Rome at same time. 1513. *Rinaldo* year (Tintoret born year before, 1512); Dürer's Knight and Death, &c.; Rafael finished the Camera della Segnatura (Stanze). 1588, Armada year. Veronese died. Velasquez born eleven years after, 1599.

CLASSICAL AND PASTORAL.
N. Poussin, 1594. Claude, 1600.

French Moderns. Bernhaim-Chardin.
L. David, Ingres, &c.

FLEMISH.
Rubens, born 1577. Vandyke.

Dutch.
Vandervelde, &c. } Dutch Realism.

Holbein, died in England 1543. Northern Master of Cinquecento.
English Ballads, Portraits and Landscape.
Hogarth, born ten years after Velasquez, 1697, died 1764.
Reynolds, born 1723, died 1788.
John (Kitchin), born 1777, died 1837.
Turner, born 1775, died 1853.

www.ingramcontent.com/pod-product-compliance
Lightning Source LLC
Chambersburg PA
CBHW022051230426
43672CB00008B/1142